What People Are Saying About Engaged!

"What do a footware company, a natural and organic food store, and a major airline have in common? Not only are they household names; they're also the same companies that understand that making the world a better place and being profitable aren't mutually exclusive. In their new book, the Volo's show us a new way of thinking: corporate success with a heart. Read their book and get *Engaged*!" **Marshall Goldsmith – the Thinkers50 Award Winner (sponsored by *Harvard Business Review*) for Most-Influential Leadership Thinker in the World**

"Karin and Sergio are absolutely on target with the right message for the right times. Doing well and doing aren't separate ideas, but in fact are the key to getting engaged and cracking The Amazing Code in the New Millennium. As we discovered in our global research, the greatest companies and leaders become the Most Admired when you understand that giving more value than you get is secret to Success Built to Last!" **Mark C. Thompson, New York Times Bestselling Author of *Admired: 21 Ways to Double Your Value* and one of the best executive coaches in the world**

"Karin and Sergio Volo have written an inspiring and helpful book that outlines the practical steps needed to develop Amazing Companies. The business world needs more focus on how positivity can transform the way we think about success and life. This uplifting book demonstrates how bringing positivity into the business world is a viable strategy to grow your business, and the Volos have first-hand experience as to how powerful these strategies can be. It's a great read for anyone wanting to make a positive difference in their lives and at work." **Shawn Achor, CEO of GoodThink Inc., author of *The Happiness Advantage*, and winner of over a dozen distinguished teaching awards at Harvard University**

i

"Recognizing your employees is just one step that can transform any company. This book is an easy and inspiring read that will make you realize it IS possible to create an amazing company and have your employees thriving." **Razor Suleman, CEO and Founder of Achievers**

"A delightful collection of valuable insights to help you succeed with a purpose driven company. This book points towards an uplifting future where learning and serving are essential to stay relevant, and to stay in business." **Ron Kaufman, New York Times bestselling author of *UPLIFTING SERVICE***

"Karin and Sergio Volo have cracked the code to creating amazing workplaces. This book is a must read for all leaders who are looking to create a highly motivated, engaged workforce. " **Kevin Kruse, author, Employee Engagement 2.0**

"Who's going to save the world? To me, it is clear that business has a vital role to play. Global problems demand global solutions and this is where businesses have the crucial role to step up and deliver. Successful companies of tomorrow will all have 'do good' in their DNA. The Volos have not only found that the answer to Amazing companies lies within their culture and their people, but they have also managed to break it down into five simple 'cultural keys' and a step by step process to get there. If you believe in the power of doing good business, this book gives you the keys you need to get there!" **Stefan Krook, serial entrepreneur, MD Kivra AB, Founder and Chairman of GodEl & GoodCause Foundation**

"The Volo's have identified some of the key ingredients that are essential to achieving sustainable business success - when the 5 C's—Collaboration, Creativity, Connection, Celebration, and Contribution—become a way of life, amazing performance will be the result." **Jennifer Rhule, Managing Director of Leadership Transformation Limited, author of *Find The Leader In You*, with over 25 years experience in HR and OD**

"Engage! lays out a road map to bring out the best in your employees. Doesn't every employee deserve to say 'Thank God It's Monday!'? Here's a plan." **Roxanne Emmerich, CEO The Emmerich Group, Inc., Best-Selling Author of *Thank God It's Monday!***

"If you believe employees should be treated like human beings rather than human resources, then you'll love this book! It's both practical and inspirational, and brings you inside GameChanging organizations that are creating truly amazing work environments." **Andrew Hewitt, Founder, GameChangers500.com**

ENGAGE!

*Your Step By Step Guide to Creating a
Workplace That You, Your Co-Workers,
and Your Customers LOVE!*

Karin & Sergio Volo

Published by A Life With A Fabulous View Inc. in collaboration with Verbii.com

1st Edition: October 2013

Paperback / Softcover ISBN
978-0-9837960-1-5
E-book ISBN
978-0-9837960-3-9
Digitised book
978-0-9837960-2-2

Copies are available at special rates for bulk orders.
Contact the sales team at sales@TheEngageBook.com

For press and media related inquiries, contact: support@Evoloshen.com

A Personal Message from Karin and Sergio:

Connect with us!

We are thrilled to share our first book with you. But more importantly, we are interested in connecting and continuing a dialogue with you. We'd love to hear what is working for you and what you may be struggling with. Please connect with us by joining our mailing list at www.Evoloshen.com and get a free gift.

You can also get daily inspiration from our Facebook page www. EvoloshenFan.com.

Bulk Purchases and Speaking

For information regarding discounts on bulk purchases, contact sales@TheEngageBook.com

To invite Karin to speak at your next event, please contact our office directly at either 1 (888) 370-9996 or +46 (0)8 5459 4460— Monday – Friday 9am-5pm (CEST) or email support@Evoloshen.com

"We must learn that doing good is good for business."

~ Sir Richard Branson

ENGAGE:

to have full attention, commitment,
enthusiasm, passion, and purpose
for your work, to be wholeheartedly
involved in and contribute positively
to an organization.

Table of Contents

Introduction

We are so glad you're holding this book in your hands right now. It means you are open minded, ready to look at a new way of doing business, and interested in how others are doing well during these very challenging economic times.

The truth is, our world is changing rapidly and it is a challenge just to keep up with it all. From technological advances to demographic changes to huge global shifts of how humanity is looking at the world, it's not surprising that many people are feeling a bit lost, overwhelmed, or out of control.

The reality is that a very high percentage of people are not engaged in their work. The statistics are staggering where over 70 percent either disengaged or actively disengaged which is costing society over $450 billion per year in lost productivity alone! If the average cost of employee turnover is 150 percent of a person's salary, and the average investment in engagement programs is at most two to three percent, then why aren't more companies investing in their people? Why aren't people a much higher priority? Southwest Airlines says that "the front line is the bottom line". They understand that investing in their employees is good for the business.

We searched for an encompassing definition of engage but didn't find one that described what we thought was sufficient. Hence, we have defined engage as doing something with full attention, commitment, enthusiasm, passion, and purpose that positively contributes to an organization. Being wholeheartedly involved is truly bringing out your best effort—it is when a person, or organization, is reaching their full potential.

We will outline in this book just how engagement or the lack thereof, is affecting companies today. We will show the alarming figures that should be raising the red flags to all leaders of companies in order to evaluate if they are on the path to truly optimizing the organization—or not. Lack of engagement is costing our societies even more than lower productivity; it is affecting our health and well being, our creativity, and even our growth as humanity. Whereas when we are engaged, we are feeling more energy, better health, there is greater innovation, jobs are created, and society is functioning at more effective levels.

This book is not for anyone who wants to maintain the status quo; who believes that things have been working just fine and wants to keep it running the way it has for years, decades, and even centuries. This book is not for someone who believes that profits are the only reason companies exists and that money is the greatest motivator of people and the world.

This book is geared towards people in business; people who are hard working and who want to make a positive difference in the world. It is for business owners, executives, entrepreneurs, and employees who know that things can be better and want to figure out how they can be proactive to make their company—and in turn, the world—a better place.

It's for people who believe in a bigger purpose and want to be a part of creating something great that has a positive impact in the world. It's for people who know that our industrial based systems are in the midst of collapsing and that new sustainable and creative solutions—experienced based models—are emerging that will support humanity and our planet; for those who want to be of service to the world, who want to know how to create Raving Fans out of their employees and customers, and who want to contribute to the wellbeing of humanity.

On the outside, our world may look crazy and very dismal. But this is a natural part of our evolution. In order to lose the old, we must examine it, release it, and then consciously choose to do things differently... to engage... and evolve. This is the first time in recorded history that we are experiencing this shift on a conscious level. We have a much larger understanding of how our world works... but we also believe that this is only the tip of the iceberg. Many more changes are in the works. We have a choice to resist this inevitable change or to embrace it.

Much of the content of this book isn't anything new—a lot of what we discuss has been around for a long time. But it has not been the main focus for companies. Many human resource directors will be glad to see that these concepts are being embraced by enlightened executives and boards.

What is new is the paradigm shift we are facing in the world and that now we, as leaders of this shift, can embrace this new mindset that focuses on employee engagement and maximizing potential in each and every person for the good of the company and the world.

We have worked with companies going through transitions for many years through our executive search business, our coaching and mentoring, and more recently, our focus on employee engagement and cultural transformation. We have survived some pretty tough times ourselves personally and we have made very deliberate choices on how to respond to challenges.

We have studied and talked to employees, executives, and founders of many companies. We've been impressed with some and other companies we know are just starting on their journey to evolve. What we have found is a new business mindset that we will explore in this book.

One interesting trend that emerged in our research is that the companies taking on the principles we discuss here are often consumer businesses, many in the retail business. We believe this to be because that is where the market is demanding it first.

The companies that are serving businesses seem to be slower to adapting to this. We have tried to find companies from various countries, different industries, large and small, publicly traded, and privately held to show that these models work in all areas. The companies that are adapting these principles are the leaders in their industry and niche—they are the game changers and the disrupters who are shaking things up. And we like that!

We are not coming from an academic approach and this book is far from an exhaustive study. It is more a collection of Amazing Companies who have discovered keys and core elements to be successful into the future and Inspiring Companies that are actively taking steps to becoming model companies. The message is strong, the principles sound, and it is our hope that you will take these concepts to heart and make a difference in your company, your work, and your personal life as well.

To our collective evolution....

Karin & Sergio Volo

August 2013

What We Believe...

- We believe in challenging the status quo.
- We believe in a new way of doing business.
- We believe in thinking differently.
- We believe in the power of the people and their passion.
- We believe in collaboration and contribution.
- We believe that joy and happiness create profitable companies that can change the course of the world.

The way we challenge the status quo is by helping companies focus in their soul and core, by making our program work from the inside out using a fun and simple methodology, and by creating a unique experience which evolves companies to Amazing Companies with Raving Fans. Want to be one?

Section One

The Foundation

1

What is the Amazing Code?

What is it that makes a company an Amazing Company? It all revolves around engagement. We believe the right combination of certain core elements allows a company to excel beyond anyone's expectations to create an environment where employees thrive and customers rave about it. We call this the Amazing Code and we'll be exploring those elements in this book.

What we are defining as an Amazing Company is very similar to a definition of humanistic companies we found in *Firms of Endearment*, an inspiring book about great companies.

> *"A humanistic company is run in such a way that its stakeholders—customers, employees, suppliers, business partners, society, and many investors— develop an emotional connection with it, an affectionate regard not unlike the way many people feel about their favorite sports team. Humanistic companies seek to maximize their value to society as a whole, not just to their shareholders. They are the ultimate value creators: They create emotional value, experiential value, social value, and of course, financial value."[1]*

The people in a company are its biggest asset. The product or service can easily be duplicated, and it will over time, but the people cannot and that is one of the essential keys that differentiate an average company from an Amazing Company. This entire book will explain the elements and how you can integrate them to engage your employees and create an Amazing Company.

Unfortunately, our school systems and our work places are often set up to be average. This has created an environment with high disengagement that is hurting our society. We rate and compare each other with the bar being set by the average. But what good is that if you want to be amazing? You need to then strive to be far above average (which often doesn't take so much extra effort).

Why should we settle for *average* in life? Especially when we can be amazing! That is really a question worth pondering over. And not from the perspective of comparing yourself or your company with others, but from the fact that we *all* can be amazing and we should be nurturing a culture of striving to be our best in all ways.

There is a journey to go from average to amazing.

In our business, we've founded our entire Evoloshen Program and System on setting the bar by the companies we have found to be amazing. These companies have a different and new approach to how they are doing business. And we believe they are on to something because their employees are much happier than average, their customers are way more satisfied than the average, and they've created a company culture that attracts the best talent. They also are quite clear on the good they are doing in the world; they exist to make our planet better in some way and that message come across very clearly in how they communicate.

One of the great business books from the last decade is *Good to Great* by Jim Collins. We often get asked if the concepts in our book are the same as the concepts in Collins' one. Our answer is that although there are some similarities, the world has changed so much since the start of the millennium. There are major global trends that are affecting all of us; this is leading to a new way of thinking in business that needs to be addressed and show-cased. That is why we've studied our model companies and have written this book.

We'll get more into some of these Amazing Companies in the scope of this book, but for now let's look at what it takes to become one of The Most Amazing Companies out there!

2

Why the New Mindset?

The Average to Amazing Journey

Going from average to amazing is a journey. It's a change of mindset and how you will look at the world. It's a shift. It is... an evolution.

Let's start with the basics.

■ Change perspective, look at what's going well instead of what's going wrong

Too often, we focus on what's wrong instead of what's right. This means that we are distracted from what we are doing well. Yes, it's important to know if you are making a mistake to avoid more of them, but ranting and raving, or beating yourself or others up for something that was done, is counterproductive to an organization and yourself.

What you focus on will expand in your life. It's a matter of reconditioning the brain by understanding how it's possible and through practicing simple exercises. This works in *all* scenarios: individuals, families, and companies. Some very small shifts in thinking can make radical changes in a person's life and in an organization.

So spend the majority of your time looking at what is going well and how you can continue to improve that.

■ Focus on your strengths instead of trying to improve where you are not so strong—spend your energy towards becoming even better

In the same light, focusing on your strengths—and knowing what they are, so you can focus on them—is essential to reaching your full potential. This is displayed best in sports. If you look at a professional athlete such as a basketball player, are they training on their golf skills because they want to improve it? Or are they spending all their time practicing their shots from the free throw line? They are, of course, spending the majority of their time on the court so that they can play an amazing game when it counts. So why should we do anything differently in business? For our professional lives, we need to understand exactly what our passions, talents, and strengths are so that we can excel in our work.

■ What are your passions, talents, and strengths? Know them and use them daily!

Through our years in executive search, it was always surprising how candidates didn't know the answers to some of these questions. Often, people would confuse strengths and talents as well, which we will define more later on in this book. People were just following a career path that they were told (by parents, teachers, supervisors, colleagues, and friends) would be best for them... without doing their own homework. And then they would wonder why their lives felt empty or were searching for the right job, one that would give them that satisfaction they were seeking. They were looking for external answers—when the answers were always within them the entire time.

■ We all want to be happy, regardless of the path we are taking to find it

> Happiness is even more than a good feeling—it is also an indispensible ingredient of our success. — *Shawn Achor, The Happiness Advantage*

Once our basic needs are met with food, shelter, and safety, we are then able to enter the pursuit of happiness. Happiness ranked just above love and health as the most important part of our lives.

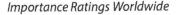

The World We All Want?

Importance Ratings Worldwide

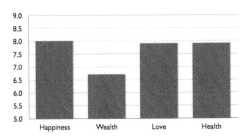

Source: Diener & Scollon 2003

In fact, March 20, 2013 (the Spring Equinox), marked the celebration of the first annual International Happiness Day as designated by the United Nations.

There is a profound shift in attitude that is underway all over the world. "People are now recognizing that 'progress' should be about increasing human happiness and wellbeing, not just growing the economy at all costs," say the organizers of the #HappyDay initiative. In the words of the UN secretary-general

7

Ban Ki-moon: "We need a new economic paradigm that recognizes the parity between the three pillars of sustainable development. Social, economic, and environmental wellbeing are indivisible. Together they define gross global happiness." [2]

The Gross National Happiness Index was first started in the early 1970s in Bhutan, a tiny Himalayan kingdom nestled high in the Himalayan mountains. Bhutan measures prosperity by gauging its citizens' happiness levels, not the GDP. Since 1971, the citizens of Bhutan have rejected GDP as the only way to measure progress. Instead, they believe that the wellbeing and happiness of the people matter and should be measured and counted. They use the formal principles of gross national happiness (GNH) and the spiritual, physical, social, and environmental health of its citizens and natural environment to evaluate their levels of prosperity. [3]

Considering that besides sleeping, the biggest bulk of time in our lives is spent working, it becomes clear how essential it is for each person to be happy at work. The statistics on the level of unhappiness at work are chilling. In general, studies show that up to 70 percent or more are not happy at work and are dreading Mondays. This is a global tragedy! Our lives are too short for us to be miserable for up to at least one third of our lives!

The benefits that come from having happy or joyful employees are huge! People tend to be more motivated and engaged in their tasks, have a higher energy level, and produce higher quality results. Having happier employees naturally leads to better customer service and interaction, lower staff turnover, less sick leave, and it makes it easier to attract others to the company. All of these have a direct impact on the bottom line—greater growth and profitability for a company.

Here's a great list as to why happy people make such a difference in the workplace.[4]

❶ Happy people work better with others

❷ Happy people are more creative

❸ Happy people fix problems instead of complaining about them

❹ Happy people have more energy

❺ Happy people are more optimistic

❻ Happy people are way more motivated

❼ Happy people get sick less often

❽ Happy people learn faster

❾ Happy people worry less about making mistakes—and consequently make fewer of them

❿ Happy people make better decisions

Some of the most successful companies on this planet, such as Microsoft, Virgin, or Google, actively work with creating a great workplace as one of their key strategic objectives. Smart leaders know this and work proactively to create an Amazing Company that others are clamoring to be a part of.

■ There is a difference between happiness and joy

There is a lot of discussion about happiness at work and how it can change an organization. There is even a "science to happiness". We'd like to clarify the definition between happiness and joy because it is often misinterpreted or misunderstood.

According to the dictionary, joy is:

- The emotion of great delight or happiness caused by something exceptionally good or satisfying; keen pleasure; elation.
- A source or cause of keen pleasure or delight; something or someone greatly valued or appreciated.

And happiness is:

- The quality or state of being happy.
- Good fortune; pleasure; contentment; joy.

They sound very similar but there are some distinct differences.

- Joy comes from within, from an inner sense of peace, as well as from enthusiasm, excitement, passion, and optimism. It is long-lasting; an attitude of the heart—a state of being.
- Happiness is external. It comes from being happy with situations and circumstances. It is more temporary in nature—a positive emotion.

Joy comes from knowing your purpose and that you are doing what you are meant to be doing. So many people feel lost in their lives simply because they are not clear on this one piece of the puzzle. When they do the inner work and get aligned with their purpose and values, suddenly clarity comes to them; it becomes much easier to make decisions, take action, and find the joy inside of them.

An entire segment of research has developed around the Science of Happiness. An acclaimed psychotherapist, Martin Seigelman, is the founder of positive psychology and the creator of the PERMA model. We find that the PERMA model encompasses *all* the elements when you have joy in your life. PERMA in short for Positive emotions, Engagement, Relationships, Meaning, and Accomplishment.[5]

- Positive emotions:
  - For us to experience wellbeing, we need positive emotions in our lives. Any positive emotion like peace, gratitude, satisfaction, pleasure, inspiration, hope, curiosity, or love falls into this category—and the message is that it's really important to enjoy yourself in the here and now.

- Engagement:
  - When we're truly engaged in a situation, task, or project, we experience a state of flow: time seems to stop, we lose our sense of self, and we concentrate intensely on the present.

- Relationships:
  - As humans, we are "social beings" and good relationships are core to our wellbeing. People who have meaningful, positive relationships with others are happier than those who do not. Relationships matter!

- Meaning:
  - Meaning comes from serving a cause bigger than ourselves. It's the way that we contribute and make a positive difference to the world. There needs to be a higher purpose to what we do and we need to know what that is.

- Accomplishment/Achievement:
  - We feel good when we have set goals and have accomplished them. This gives us the road map to do what we do and to measure it by whatever standards we give it. We can think big with our dreams, break it down into smaller goals, and then plan the action steps to accomplish what we set out to do.

Whether you choose to focus on happiness or joy isn't so relevant because they are so similar. But finding joy is a longer-lasting state of being, not dependent on the external circumstances. It comes from within and therefore is a deeper and more authentic way of living. It is important to note though that happy employees are not necessarily engaged employees, something we will delve into extensively.

What we find fascinating is that there are companies embracing the concept of Joy. BMW did a marketing campaign in the UK about the joy of driving. And PUMA has joy as part of their entire brand strategy. This is from their press kit:

*"We are the brand that remembers what it was like to play the game – and to play it with joy. It's what we've always done best and now the time is right to bring the joy back again. So when we think about product, about marketing, retail or anything in our business, the first question we must ask is: Where is the Joy? It could be the feeling of running fast on a track, or getting social with your friends playing ping pong at a bar. **Joy is being the best while having fun doing it.**"*

The highlight is our emphasis. Bringing joy into the workplace is a trend that is happening in many ways.

■ You have control over your life!

When we work with individuals and groups, we teach them how to "reframe" events (either past, current, or future ones), which essentially shows them how to look at it from a different perspective. When someone realizes that they have more control and understanding of how they can influence their own emotions, it's like they've been given the keys to happiness. Our brains get conditioned to seeing the world through certain filters based on our experiences and early programming during childhood.

The bad news is that we are very often not even aware of the programs subconsciously running our lives. However, the exciting news is that this is not permanent. You can change your brain and conditioning, and there are a number of excellent ways to do so. Becoming a more joyful, happier person is possible for anyone! We show others how to change their perspective in viewing the world from conditioned negative tendencies to a more positive outlook. What you focus on is what you will see in your life.

Imagine that you are skiing downhill through some trees. Instead of being afraid of hitting the trees, focus on the spaces between the trees and you'll glide through the forest. When you change your focus from being afraid to hit the trees to going through the space between the trees, you'll get down the mountain unscathed. Life works in the same way!

3

Why Engagement Is A Critical Business Strategy In Today's Market

Engagement has become a hot topic. It is important to view it from many perspectives to understand how it truly impacts an organization. Because people make up the essence of any company, we must look at how engagement relates to both retention of employees and the attraction of talent.

Retention

Retaining your top talent is crucial in the coming years. There are four critical talent issues most companies are facing now: managing a global workforce, competing for leaders with the right skills, an aging workforce and identifying, developing and retaining future leaders. A new report, *The Business Impact of Talent Intelligence*, released by the Human Capital Institute with talent management company <u>Taleo</u>, examines the connections between financial performance and what it calls, the use of "talent intelligence," which drives innovation and performance.[6]

Even with the streamlining of organizations and the high rates of unemployment in so many countries, there is still, and always will be, a demand for top talent. Let's face it, the people who over-deliver will always be attractive.

Most people think someone makes a job change because of a better position or a higher salary. Surprisingly, those are often NOT the primary reasons. After years of recruiting top talent from companies and interviewing thousands of people ready to make a job change, there are three most common reasons as to why most people will start seeking new opportunities.

One is because they are searching for something outside of themselves, only they do not realize that. They want to be happier and think that a new job will give them that boost up—and it often will...for a while. However, if someone hasn't done their "inner work" first, they will continue to search externally and not be 100% engaged or committed. Sooner or later, this will eventually lead into a downward spiral effect in their lives, at least in terms of their level of happiness and well being.

The second most common reason for wanting to make a change is that there is a cultural or personality mismatch, either with the company, the team they worked with, or their supervisor. Poor management drives top talent away which in turn has a significant impact on the bottom line. When the culture or personality is not a fit, employees start to look elsewhere. Again, they are seeking to find more stability and happiness outside of themselves.

The third motivator for making a change is that they want to be a part of something bigger. They want to feel like they are contributing on a significant level and are on a mission to transform or be a part of transforming a company. Since so many of the companies we headhunted for were in the midst of a major transition, that may be why we saw a high percentage of people who were ready to become a part of something significant. However, the future trends show that contributing to a larger purpose and making a difference are becoming more important to individuals.

Even if someone is making a job change because they want that promotion to climb the corporate ladder, the true inner drivers tend to be buried deeply emotionally as to why this is important to them. And it often takes years of hard work, ambition, and sacrifices before some sort of crisis comes to shake their foundation and makes them re-evaluate what is truly important in their lives.

It is essential for a person to understand what really motivates them, what makes them feel passionate and charged about their work, and what gives them a sense of purpose. When someone has not taken the time to do this inner searching, they tend to go from one job to another and although their career path may seem right on the outside, on the inside, they become farther and farther removed from their true purpose. This leads to mid-life crisis, depression, lack of motivation, and a sense of loss of identity. It's a common crisis that many executives and professionals face at some point in their lives.

High employee turnover for a company is a huge underlying problem that is not so tangible, making it more difficult to address. Many companies do not have systems in place to measure the true costs and the indirect costs are much higher than most would think.

Individually, it costs between $4,000-$14,000 to replace an hourly employee, and upwards to $40,000 to replace a manager. One Silicon Valley company estimates the cost of replacing an employee is over $125,000.[7]

While many leading companies place more effort on employee retention, many remain clueless. They accept employee turnover as a normal part of doing business. High turnover organizations spend disproportionate amounts of resources on recruiting and replacing their workforce, while smart organizations invest in employee retention.

The turnover replacement costs by industry. (U.S. dollars) per employee:

- Construction $14,500
- Manufacturing $14,500
- Trade & Transportation $12,500
- Information $19,500
- Financial Activities $18,000
- Professional & Business $15,500
- Education & Health $14,000
- Leisure & Hospitality $7,000
- Other Services $12,750
- All Private $14,000

Source: Employment Policy Foundation tabulation and analysis of Bureau of Labor Statistics, Employer Cost of Employee Compensation data.

Yes, there is going to be employee turnover no matter what you do, but blindly ignoring the reasons—and NOT actively working towards improving retention—shows a lack of foresight and is an expensive mistake.

When the turnover statistics are high in an organization, it is a huge cost for a company. Figures show that the cost of employee turnover will easily reach 150% of the employee's annual compensation figure. This cost will be significantly higher (200% to 250% of annual compensation) for managerial and sales positions.[8]

To put this into perspective, let's assume the average salary of employees in a given company is $50,000 per year. Taking the cost of turnover at 150% of salary, the cost of turnover is then $75,000 per employee who leaves the company. For the mid-sized company of 1,000 employees who has a 10% annual rate of turnover, the annual cost of turnover is $7.5 million! This includes:

- Costs due to person leaving
- Recruitment costs (both internal and external)
- Training costs
- Lost productivity costs
- New hire costs
- Lost sales costs

Therefore, it is very cost effective for a company to invest in the retention of its staff and developing people within the organization. The return on investment on the development and retention of staff can range anywhere from 30 percent to 7000 percent, depending on the parameters chosen to measure.[9]

To keep the figures conservative, we'll say the average ROI is 30 percent—but keep in mind, we are so not striving for average here either! We're aiming for amazing! Regardless, there are countless studies that prove an effective strategy to increase profits and productivity are to actively work with retaining and developing great employees. The investment into an employee engagement or recognition program can be anywhere from one to three percent of an employee's annual salary. How much is employee turnover and lack of engagement costing your organization? How much is it worth to you to improve the performance of your staff, to develop new talent, and retain top talent?

With the Evoloshen System, the steps are mapped out in a way that is easy to follow and implement within an organization. Whether you choose to follow this system or work on your own, taking the decision to invest the time, money, and effort to creating an Amazing Company—that is a highly engaged organization, is the first step to reaching new levels of business that will far exceed your expectations.

Let's explore the flip side to retention, which is attraction.

Attraction

In order to understand the importance of attraction, we need to look at the current climate of the workplace in the world.

- **Even with high unemployment, talent is still hard to recruit.**
  - 60% of North American companies are having trouble attracting critical-skill employees.[10]
- **Talent shortages and mismatches are impacting profitability now.**
  - One in four CEOs said they were unable to pursue a market opportunity or have had to cancel or delay a strategic initiative because of talent challenges.
  - One in three is concerned that skills shortages will impact their company's ability to innovate effectively.
  - Skills shortages are seen as a top threat to business expansion.[11]
- **Discontented employees are starting to look elsewhere.**
  - In a survey by global business consulting firm Right Management, 84 percent of the employees polled said they plan to look for a new position in 2012.[12]
  - An American Psychological Association survey found that half of all employees who do not feel "valued" at work, intend to bolt.[13]

If you are not alarmed by these statistics, you should be. The world is shifting rapidly in many ways and companies need to keep up with the changes to stay in the game. The only way to do this is through the people working in the company. And that means being able to not only attract the best talent, but also keep them for a longer time.

Another important consideration is that the hiring process is a sales process, not a buying process. It is essential that the company is able to present itself in a way that top talent buys into wanting to come work there. We cannot even count how many companies went into a recruitment process with an attitude that of course, everyone would want to work there. Even if it is a desirable company to work for, there must be a great match with many factors, such as culture and personality fit, personal chemistry between the team or supervisor, values and mission, goals and long term growth opportunities, etc. It is a sales process from start to finish and must be treated as such in order to get the best talent.

However, once an Amazing Company status is reached, the attraction process changes again to one of mutual choice and a "marriage". There is an element of internal knowing from both sides that this would be an excellent match. We believe this comes from having the knowledge and ability to express the common values, passions, and purpose that are in alignment with each other.

When a company has created a Thriving Culture, they have a Magnetic Tribe. People are drawn to the company. Customers start to look at the company as a place they would love to work as well. When the employees are also Raving Fans, they help to recruit some of the best talent available. When the internal work in the organization starts to fall into place, the external aspects of attraction also become easier to work with. We will delve deeper into the factors that help to create this through our two models discussed in this book and share how the Evoloshen System is an encompassing approach to creating an Amazing Company.

Before we take you there, we first need to examine the current global trends and disruptive changes that are affecting everyone.

4

Global Trends and Disruptive Change

■ **The world is changing quickly and it's not changing linearly, but exponentially, due to technological advances**

We are trained to think linearly. But our world is changing at a much faster rate now than ever before. For example, in a single day, we take in an estimated 174 newspapers worth of information! That is an increase of over 400 percent from thirty years ago when it was approximately only forty newspapers worth of data per day.[14]

Technology has certainly made it easier to communicate globally, but there is a lot of noise out there, something that is essential for companies to understand in order to get through to their customers.

"The value in today's economy is principally knowledge and information, whether information is a movie, music, or a piece of software, or some inventory control database. This trend will continue in an exponential way." – Ray Kurzweil, renowned futurist[15]

We've also made a change from the Age of Information to the Age of Transformation and that entails an evolution in the way we do things.

This change has happened so fast that most people are not even aware we have entered into a new era, and that's due to the rapidly changing technological advances and the change in mindset humanity is experiencing.

- In the last decade, there have been more than one billion new users online and more than four billion new people using cell phones.
- There are huge technological advancements as products get smarter, faster, and cheaper to produce, making them much more accessible for everyone.
- There is also a trend of dematerializing industries as technological advances surge, making products and services obsolete. (Just look at what has happened to the music industry in the last decade.)

We need to adapt quickly. The Internet has revolutionized the way we do business. We are connected globally 24/7. This means we have access to customers at all times and we can work from anywhere at any time.

Technological advances have always driven disruptive change in the workplace. In the nineteenth century, the Industrial Age moved workers from an agricultural to a production model.

In the twentieth century, we experienced another revolution as the Information Age moved workers from factories into offices.

In the twenty first century, we are in the midst of a virtual Transformation Age where the Internet and technology are redefining our workplace yet again.

Work is becoming much more collaborative as communication makes it easy to stay connected.

People need to take their education into their own hands and make sure they stay relevant in the changing market place. They are beginning to understand that they are in control of their own future and must manage their own careers based on what they are passionate about and naturally talented to do so that they can easily succeed.

■ Demographic changes

There are now four generations in the workforce, all with different generational traits.[16] They include the silent generation (1922-45), the baby boomers (1946-64), generation X (1965-80) and generation Y (1981-onward). Each generation has its own values, work style, and management style.

Generational Traits in the Workplace			
Silent generation	Baby boomers	Generation X	Generation Y
This generation is hardworking, trusting, optimistic, and very moral.	This generation is optimistic and driven to succeed in a work environment.	This generation is not very trusting, but very adaptable to change. Has a good idea of work and life balance.	This generation is hard working and adaptable to change. Optimistic about the future and open to ideas.

This has caused challenges with management and working together due to the lack of understanding and due to the generations not being aligned in values with one another. We also have older generations that are working longer; at the same time, there is a mass exodus in the workforce as workers in their sixties are retiring.

Generational Values in the Workplace			
Silent generation	**Baby boomers**	**Generation X**	**Generation Y**
Dedication	Optimism	Diversity	Civic duty
Hard work	Team focus	World thought	Confidence
Respect	Health	Balance	Optimism
Conformity	Personal growth	Fun	Social ability
Duty	Work	Self-reliance	Morality
Delayed gratification	Involvement	Technologically literate	Achievement

How is this going to impact business and our future? How are you prepared to ride the wave of change that has already started? And do you have an understanding of the different engagement strategies that work for various generations?

Many governments are looking to raise the retirement age from sixty five to sixty seven—and even seventy—as people are living longer and the retirement programs and systems cannot support the mass influx of retirees at the same time. On one hand, this is good because people want to feel needed or valued, and forced retirement often brings about depression and a loss of purpose. On the other hand, it can be quite difficult for older workers to get new employment or make any job changes at this stage in life. We're seeing a high percentage of people aged fifty and above starting their own companies as well. This is something we call "forced entrepreneurship", when someone needs to create their own work. This is a generation that tends to be more engaged, likely due to the fact that their families are grown and they have more time to focus on work.

On the other side of the age spectrum, we see a new workforce coming that looks at the world from a whole different perspective. According to the *Harvard Business Review*, by 2014, the

Millennials—those born between 1977 and 1997—will account for half of all the employees in the world. This generation is not at all motivated by money. They are very purpose and value driven and are very selective on what companies they will work for. They cannot be wooed by high salaries, fancy cars, or bonuses, but rather look for companies with bigger purposes: the ones making a positive difference in the world. This is also the generation most likely to make a job change in the next twelve months.

In the middle, we have the generations that are least engaged currently. College educated, middle aged employees are the group that is least giving their full attention to their employers. This could be in part because of the pressures they are facing with raising their families as well as taking care of elder parents. They have also experienced many rounds of layoffs in recent years which may also be affecting their level of commitment and enthusiasm at their workplace.

Employers need to understand the changing trends so that they can become more flexible to meet the requirements of the talents they need to retain in order to succeed. They need to manage workers living all over the world. They need to understand the value of life-work integration and to offer flexible options that allow workers to produce the required results. And they need to be very clear on a bigger purpose as to why they are in business. They must take actions to transform their employees and their customers into their Raving Fans by creating a deeper and more purposeful relationship with them.

Understanding this huge shift... this time of disruptive change, and knowing how to navigate during this time, will make the difference in extinction, survival, or thriving for companies.

■ The Most Amazing Company Strategy

Historically, the way we measure standards is based on the average—from school to work, we've been conditioned to see what the average is and then strive to be average like everyone else.

But we don't start there.

We have built our Evoloshen Program and System—and The Most Amazing Company strategy—around the best of the best companies doing the most innovative practices to date.

When we measure customer satisfaction or employee satisfaction, what are we really measuring? The definition for satisfy is as follows: *to fulfill the desires, expectations, needs, or demands of (a person, the mind, etc.); give full contentment.*

Satisfaction is the same as OK or fine—but there is no WOW in that!

We are striving to far exceed satisfaction with EXCELLENCE—the WOW factor.

What makes a company amazing is that they have Raving Fans—they far exceed the average and over-deliver; they exceed the expectations of their customers, partners, suppliers, employees, and contribution to the world.

They deliver the WOW factor:

- Word of mouth advertising is the best and strongest kind of advertising that will have a much better and lasting impact.
- The word spreads through social media because we are living in a transparent society (and traditional marketing avenues simply are not producing what they used to).

- Over-deliver on the experience and expectations for your products and services for everyone involved with the company.
- Create a culture that everyone wants to be a part of.
- Even when you make mistakes, your fans will be very forgiving and are rooting to see you succeed!
- Have a higher purpose for making the world a better place in some way that is clear and consistent in your message and marketing.
- When you have created this, you do not need to sell because the message sells itself and, if the marketing is done correctly, pre-sells your customers before they even come to you!
- You do not need to worry about competition because who is going to take you away from your higher purpose? People will want to help you reach your objectives.
- Your profits increase because your employees are more productive. You have higher repeat business from your customers.

What business owner doesn't want this for their business? What leaders wouldn't love to have this environment to work with? What employees wouldn't love to be part of making such a difference in the world? The great news is that this is possible for any business—if you're willing to do the work to get there.

This will mean turning some things upside down from the traditional ways of doing business. It means being open minded and willing to embrace new ways of thinking and of seeing the world. It means taking the leadership role of implementing the change. But the upside to this is far greater than the uncomfortable space of change.

We all need to embrace the changes our world is facing and allow the best of the best of these changes to surface in our lives and in the way we interact with each other. Business is still about relationships. By embracing the new technological advances, you can create quality relationships and loyalty with millions of customers.

Beyond this, Evoloshen is not about change but about transformation and evolving. Our system is structured so that it's possible to make a smoother transition; one that wouldn't be resisted by the employees but rather embraced with excitement to make this shift.

Evoloshen is the bridge between our old ways of thinking and the new emerging paradigm.

It is possible to create a market space with no competition! Evoloshen shows you how to do just that. Instead of falling into the scarcity model of thinking and going into a commodity downward spiral, we show you how to focus on the transformation and uniqueness that creates an abundant upward spiral of greater productivity and profits that benefit everyone.

It's time to shift the way we do business. The fact that you are reading this book says that you are ready to be a part of the new way of doing so.

You are ready to be a part of the solution!

5

Overview of Amazing Companies and Inspiring Companies

Here are the companies we have studied and are using as examples. We've included a brief description to give you an idea of what they are doing. Many are well known brands and others are not. As we mentioned, we have tried to get a broad range of companies, from private to public, small to large, in various geographic locations.

There are certainly hundreds of other companies that would qualify as Amazing Companies, and it is our hope that all will be inspired in taking action to start their journey as well.

Overview of Amazing Companies	
TOMS	John Lewis
Virgin	Achievers
Zappos	Patagonia
HCL Technologies	Ben & Jerry's
PUMA	ElectraWinds
Whole Foods	Misty's Dance
Southwest Airlines	W.L. Gore & Associates
MindValley	

Overview of Inspiring Companies	
Google	Choice Hotels
Apple	GodEl
Microsoft	Indiska
IKEA	Proffice
Philips	I:CO
Nordstroms	Costco
Facebook	Young and Raw
Instagram	

TOMS: A unique company with a brand of shoes where for every pair of shoes purchased, a pair of shoes is given to a child in need. Founded in 2006, out of his apartment, Blake Mycoskie, author of *Build Something That Matters*, has created a company with a soul that keeps on giving. TOMS, short for tomorrow's shoes, has also expanded into sunglasses and other products using the same model. Their contribution is built directly into their business model and it has been working great. TOMS' giving partners are made up of NGOs, charity groups, and non-profit organizations already established and working in the countries in which TOMS gives. Their expertise guides TOMS to give new shoes responsibly, making sure there aren't adverse socioeconomic effects, and ensuring that sustainable giving is possible. Giving shoes to the same children on a regular basis is the idea upon which TOMS was started, and is what truly improves the lives of children and their communities. They have grown to 160-plus employees in 2012 and have giving projects in South America and Asia. In 2007, TOMS was honored with the prestigious People's Design Award from the Cooper-Hewitt National Design Museum, Smithsonian Institution. Two years later, Blake and TOMS received the 2009 ACE award by Secretary of State, Hillary Clinton, which recognizes companies' commitment to corporate social responsibility, innovation, exemplary practices, and democratic values worldwide.

Virgin: One of the strongest global brands with over 250 companies in many markets and industries. Founded by Sir Richard Branson, who recently wrote *Screw Business As Usual* and also started the Elders (a small group of independent global leaders, including Nelson Mandela, who work together for peace and human rights), the Virgin Group has gone on to grow successful businesses in sectors, ranging from mobile telephony, travel, financial services, leisure, music, holidays, and health and wellness. Across its companies, Virgin employs approximately 50,000 people in 34 countries. Virgin believes in making a difference. They stand for value for money, quality, innovation, fun, and a sense of competitive challenge. They strive to achieve this by empowering their employees to continually deliver an unbeatable customer experience. Having fun and getting results is deeply ingrained into their culture, as well as giving back. Virgin Unite is the foundational arm of the Virgin Group and supports young entrepreneurs through the Branson Centers for Entrepreneurship in South Africa and the Caribbean. They also support a number of other initiatives that help with the environment, health issues, youth, and homelessness, and are a hub for inspired leaders and businesses.

Zappos: The largest online shoe and apparel shop grossing over $1 billion in sales with 1,800 employees, Zappos is well known for its amazing culture and customer service, using a loyalty business model and relationship-marketing to create Raving Fans. It was founded in 1999 by Nick Swinmurn and brought to a household name by entrepreneur and CEO Tony Hsieh, who also wrote *Delivering Happiness*. Zappos was bought by Amazon in 2009, and in 2010 it was restructured into ten separate companies under the Zappos Family umbrella. Their goal is to position Zappos as the online service leader. Since customers now associate the Zappos brand with the absolute best service, they are expanding into other product categories.

31

HCL Technologies: The largest "startup" in the world with over 93,000 employees, this publicly traded company is an IT Services provider that threw out traditional business models in 2007 and decided to put employees first and their customers second. This resulted in an annual growth of over 25 percent during some of the toughest economic times, when most companies were struggling. They accomplished this through trust and transparency and by empowering the front line employees. With their headquarters in India, they have offices in 31 countries and are providing IT services to many of the largest global companies. In the Nordic region, after a few short years of entering the market, they were voted by KPMG as the most innovative IT Services provider and have won numerous awards.

PUMA: Founded in 1948 in Germany, PUMA has grown to be a leading company with the objective of being "The Most Desirable and Sustainable Sport Lifestyle Company". They are committed to working in ways that contribute to the world, by supporting creativity, sustainability, and peace, and by staying true to the values of being Fair, Honest, Positive, and Creative in decisions made and actions taken. PUMA has over 11,000 employees in a decentralized organization, with four main offices in Germany, the US, the UK, and Hong Kong. The foundation for their activities is **PUMAVision**—a concept that guides their work with its three core programs: PUMA.Creative (which supports artists and organizations collaborating with creative efforts); PUMA.Safe (which is committed for environmental protection and improved working conditions and sustainable systems); and PUMA.Peace (which promotes peace awareness in the world through sports activities)._

Whole Foods: A dynamic leader in the quality food business that started in the US—and now also is in the UK market— Whole Foods is a mission-driven company that aims to set the standards of excellence for food retailers. "Quality is a state of mind at Whole Foods Market." Their motto—Whole Foods, Whole People, Whole Planet—emphasizes that their vision reaches far beyond being just a food retailer. The original Whole Foods Market opened in 1980 with a staff of only nineteen people. Now, with more than 340 stores in North America and the UK, 92 percent of their 53,000-plus employees are full-time team members. Their success in fulfilling their vision is measured by customer satisfaction, team member excellence and happiness, return on capital investment, improvement in the state of the environment, and local and larger community support.

Southwest Airlines: This is a company that has been leading a new era in commercial aviation with low fares and fun, with what they call a "maverick spirit". Southwest Airlines is America's largest low-fare carrier, serving more customers domestically than any other airline, with a unique combination of low fares with no annoying fees, friendly customer service delivered by outstanding people, safe and reliable operations, and an extraordinary corporate culture that extends into the communities they serve. Founded in 1971, Southwest continues to differentiate itself from other carriers through their focus on exemplary customer service, delivered by nearly 46,000 employees to more than 100 million customers each year among 97 destinations in 41 US states.

MindValley: MindValley is an international group of visionaries, rebels, crazed inventors, best-selling authors, quirky artists, and ambitious entrepreneurs working on pushing humanity forward through culture hacking and revolutionizing the global education system. They build new better models that make today's problematic models obsolete; and at the heart of their approach is "culture hacking", which is the art of bringing in technology and education in smart effective ways to rapidly "recode" and advance culture, altering in the process the behaviors of every-day individuals to make them adopt smarter practices that elevate their lives. Founded in 2003 by Vishen Lakhiani, this online company has grown to approximately 100 employees from 31 different countries.

John Lewis: The John Lewis Partnership is a visionary and successful way of doing business, boldly putting the happiness of partners (AKA employees) at the center of everything it does. It's the embodiment of an ideal; the outcome of nearly a century of endeavor to create a different sort of company, owned by partners dedicated to serving customers with flair and fairness. With over 69,000 partners and founded in 1864, this UK retail company is the "oldest" of our model companies. It was a revolutionary idea to start profit-sharing back in 1920. By 1928 when the founder's son, John Spendan Lewis, gained sole control of the company, he established a trust that gave full ownership to the employees. He understood that happy employees contributed to building a good, and profitable, business—an idea that has been a proven strategy for John Lewis for almost 100 years now.

Achievers: This is a company changing the way the world works. They help companies recognize and reward positive employee behaviors, resulting in higher employee engagement and better business results. With their award-winning technology, excellent customer service, and industry-leading expertise, they have powered the world's most successful rewards and recognition programs. Founded by Razor Suleman in 2002, this Canadian based company, with its approximately 200 employees, has won numerous awards and has expanded into the US, servicing corporate clients globally with their unique software and platform for recognition that fosters employee success.

Patagonia: An innovative retail company with a passion for outdoor sports and living. Patagonia was founded in 1974 by Yvon Chouinard. As they state so well on their site:

"For us at Patagonia, a love of wild and beautiful places demands participation in the fight to save them, and to help reverse the steep decline in the overall environmental health of our planet. We donate our time, services and at least 1% for our sales to hundreds of grassroots environmental groups all over the world who work to help reverse the tide. We use recycled polyester in many of our clothes and only organic, rather than pesticide-intensive, cotton."

This niched outdoor/sports company of over 1,300 employees has been concerned about environmental issues since they started forty years ago.

Ben & Jerry's: It is a high-end, high-quality ice cream manufacturer that believes business has a responsibility to give back to the community. They say that they "make the best possible ice cream in the nicest way possible". What makes Ben & Jerry's a long-lasting company making a positive impact is the people. In business over 25 years, they were purchased by Unilever in 2000 and are the only brand under Unilever's 400-plus brands that have their own board of directors and continue to keep their culture intact. They are essentially a company within a company. They believe in supporting grass roots movements that support the environment and the planet. Their Foundation awards about $1.8 million annually to eligible organizations across the country and in Vermont. Their philanthropy is solely employee led, by non-management employee advisory groups who consider proposals and recommend grants.

Electrawinds: Electrawinds is an international company based in Belgium that produces, sells, and distributes green power generated from inexhaustible clean energy resources such as wind, sun, and organic matter. Apart from constructing and operating windmill farms, solar farms, and biomass plants,

Electrawinds also investigates and develops new renewable energy possibilities and applications. The company was founded in 1998, has 230 employees, and operates in 12 countries. It became listed on the Frankfurt Stock Exchange in September 2012.

Misty's Dance Unlimited: *More Than Just Great Dancing*™! What began as a small dance studio in 1998 is now taking the dance studio experience to a new level by creating a higher purpose that builds self-confidence in their students and gives back in all that they do through their foundations and charitable events. Misty Lown is one of the most energetic entrepreneurs we have encountered, who is creating a group of companies and is innovating the dance world by fusing customer service, creating Raving Fans through a WOW experience, and bringing a solid business system to help creative dance studio owners build a profitable business for themselves.

W.L. Gore & Associates: Founders Bill and Vieve Gore started W. L. Gore & Associates in the basement of their home in 1958. This company has made its name by creating innovative, technology-driven solutions, from medical devices that treat aneurysms to high-performance GORE-TEX® fabrics. A privately held company with annual sales of more than $3.2 billion, Gore is committed to perpetuating its 50-plus year tradition of product innovation. Gore focuses its efforts in four main areas: electronics, fabrics, industrial and medical products. Today, with more than 10,000 employees (called associates) worldwide, the company is owned by members of the Gore family and associates. Gore prefers this private ownership and believes this reinforces a key element of its culture to "take a long term view" when assessing business situations. They work hard at maximizing individual potential, maintaining an emphasis on product integrity, and cultivating an environment where creativity can flourish. A fundamental belief in their people and their abilities continues to be the key to their success.

Inspiring Companies Doing Good Things

Google: Starting from two computer science students in a university dorm room in 1996, Google now has over 24,000 employees and offices around the world. They began by offering search in a single language and have expanded by offering dozens of products and services—including various forms of advertising and web applications for all kinds of tasks—in scores of languages. They are dedicated to their users and have a strong belief in the possibilities of the internet itself. Google's mission is to organize the world's information and make it universally accessible and useful.

Apple: Great ideas have a way of becoming great products, services, and customer experiences very quickly. Founded in 1976 by Steve Jobs, Apple looks for people to bring passion and dedication to their jobs with high expectations of delivering results. Apple led the digital music revolution with its iPods and iTunes online store. It has reinvented the mobile phone with its revolutionary iPhone and App Store and is defining the future of mobile media and computing devices with its iPad. With 72,000 employees globally, innovation and design are at the core of Apple's corporate DNA.

Microsoft: Microsoft believes in helping people and businesses throughout the world to realize their full potential. This simple mission comes to life every day through their passion to create technologies and to develop products that touch just about every kind of customer. Every successful corporation has a responsibility to use its resources and influence to make a positive impact on the world and its people. Microsoft's Global Citizenship Initiative is focused on mobilizing its resources across the company and around the world to create opportunities in the communities where it is doing business and to fulfill its commitment to serving the public good through innovative technologies and partnerships. Founded 1975 by Bill Gates, they now have more than 94,000 employees in over 100 countries; only a small percentage of the global population hasn't been touched yet by Microsoft in some way.

IKEA: This global company has a vision to create a better everyday life for people. Their business idea supports this vision by offering a wide range of well-designed, functional homes, furnishing products at prices so low that as many people as possible could afford them. The company is known for its modern architectural designs on various types of appliances and furniture, often associated with a simplified eco-friendly interior design. Founded in Sweden in 1943 by 17-year-old Ingvar Kamprad, it has grown to over 120,000 employees with over 300 stores in 41 countries in 4 continents. This company believes in taking care of people and the planet—from tackling the problem of children living in poverty to creating renewable energy. The IKEA Foundation supports long and short-term projects that give children a better start in life. 100 million children will benefit from current programs.

Philips: Royal Philips Electronics of the Netherlands is a diversified health and wellbeing company, focused on improving people's lives through timely innovations. As a world leader in healthcare, lifestyle, and lighting, Philips integrates technologies and design into people-centric solutions, based on fundamental customer insights and the brand promise of "sense and simplicity". The Philips Center for Health & Wellbeing is dedicated to improving people's quality of life around the world by identifying barriers to health and wellbeing and to developing solutions of overcoming these barriers. This company has approximately 118,000 employees and dates its origins back to 1891.

Nordstroms: Nordstrom's motto is "a relentless drive to exceed expectations". For more than 100 years, Nordstrom has worked to deliver the best possible shopping experience, helping customers possess style—not just buy fashion. Since 1901, they have been committed to providing their customers with the best possible service—and to improving it every day. They believe fashion is a business of optimism, and they continue to grow and evolve. Fashion and shopping changes but their commitment to happy customers doesn't. They empower their employees to set their sights high. With an employment of over 52,000 strong, they trust their employees to use their best judgment in all situations.

Facebook: Facebook's mission is to make the world more open and connected. The second most visited website in the world, they crossed one billion active users—a seventh of the planet—in September 2012. With just over 4,600 employees and roughly 1,000 engineers, each engineer is "responsible" for one million users. Founded by Mark Zuckerberg while studying at Harvard in 2004, it has grown to be the largest hub for social networking. Going public in 2012, and dropping its share price to almost half, took its toll, but the company is still growing and has created the world's largest, most efficient data-crunching machine. They believe in taking a long-term perspective to continue servicing billions of users.

Instagram: This subsidiary company, purchased by Facebook in 2012 after a short 18 months from starting with only 13 employees, offers a fun and quirky way to share your life with friends through a series of pictures. Snap a photo with your mobile phone then choose a filter to transform the image into a memory to keep around forever. They are building Instagram to allow you to experience moments in your friends' lives through pictures as they happen. They imagine a world more connected through photos and see the potential to change the world for the better. This company is combining photography with innovative technology to connect people through sharing experiences, information, and creativity.

Nordic Choice Hotels: Scandinavia's largest hotel chain franchise with 170 hotels and 9,250 employees in Scandinavia and the Baltic States. Started in 1996, this company focuses on the customer experience and in creating a passionate culture. In Nordic Choice, they have high goals and a broad engagement. Therefore, they measure success based on three different points: economic performance, environmental and social responsibility. Nordic Choice pays a voluntary carbon tax for every guest staying with them. The money will benefit the Rainforest Foundation. They believe in taking responsibility outside the hotel and into the local communities, whether it is to serve food to the local homeless or to organize a marathon for UNICEF.

GodEl: This Swedish electric company was founded by entrepreneur Stefan Krook in 2005, with the sole purpose of giving back. The idea of creating a company that gave 100 percent of its profits was a challenge he set out to prove could work. Since they were founded in 2005 to 2012, they have contributed over $3 million to various charities and have won awards for the best customer service. The company is fully owned by a non-profit foundation and distributes the profits to right different organizations. The business model clearly works and they have plenty of Raving Fans, both with their 30-70 employees (they hire 30-40 students in the summer months to connect with customers) and their 100,000-plus customers.

Indiska: A Swedish family enterprise that has existed for over 110 years with approximately 700 employees, Indiska sells fashion, interior home products and accessories with a modern, unique stamp in 90 shops in Sweden, Norway, Finland, and online. They have always been conscientious about taking responsibility, both when it comes to the world we live in and for their customers. They have very strong relationships with their suppliers, where their code of conduct is the key to change and improvement. They believe that responsible free trade is, in the long run, the best contribution to economic development and reduced social injustice in their production countries.

Proffice: This is one of the largest specialist companies within staffing and recruitment in the Nordic region, with approximately 1,000 employees and 9,000 contract employees. Founded in the 1960s in Sweden, this company has become a leading services company that understands the value of its people. They contribute to the growth and development of people and businesses through their high degree of attentiveness and their passionate commitment. Their motto "keep improving" is to inspire them to keep finding the best ways to deliver results.

I:CO: The Swiss company, I:Collect AG, part of the SOEX Group, is behind I:CO. SOEX is a world leader in the classic areas of textile and shoe recycling. With almost 2,300 employees worldwide, the corporation currently processes around 500 tons of used items every day in 74 countries. I:CO has collection points all over Europe, the USA, and Japan. In addition to the existing markets, the system is to be expanded to take on Asia, Australia, and Africa in the coming years. All players involved in I:CO are making a contribution to the environment and society. Those who join in help to prevent millions of tons of valuable raw material from being simply tossed in the garbage. For every returned kilogram of clothing, linen, or shoes, the I:CO partner companies also donate two eurocents to the CharityStar fund. Once 1,000 Euros has been reached, this sum is paid out to a charitable project. Implementing good ideas themselves and helping to get other good ideas moving is the I:CO philosophy.

Costco: This company is a membership-only warehouse club that provides a wide selection of merchandise. As of July 2012, it was the second largest retailer in the United States, with 174,000 employees and over 68 million members (customers). The company's first location opened in 1976 under the Price Club name. Founded by James (Jim) Sinegal and Jeffrey H. Brotman in 1983, the first Costco warehouse location was opened in Seattle. It became the first company ever to grow from zero to $3 billion in sales in less than six years. Costco and Price Club merged in 1993. Costco's operating philosophy has been simple: keep costs down and pass the savings on to members through lower prices. Their large membership base and tremendous buying power, combined with their never-ending quest for efficiency, result in the best possible prices for their members. Since resuming the Costco name in 1997, the company has grown worldwide with over 625 warehouses in 8 countries.

Young and Raw: Beginning as a Facebook page and as a blog, inspired from a passion of learning about nutrition and eating raw foods, Young and Raw has turned into a thriving online business by millennium entrepreneurs and co-founders Caleb Jennings and Sheleana Breakell that is transforming the lives of hundreds of thousands of people. After two years, they developed a seven-figure business with a small team of dedicated experts and employees who believe in making a difference. Their biggest draw is their "Free 30 Day Green Smoothie Challenge" which attracted thousands of participants in one month from 82-plus countries alone. They give 30 unique recipes made from fresh fruits and vegetables to try each day, which teach people that the simple practice of adding green smoothies to your daily diet can boost your energy levels, strengthen your immune system, cleanse toxins from your body, help you lose weight, help you sleep and handle stress better, and overall contribute to your health and wellbeing. They strive to educate on overall optimal wellness. We included Young and Raw because, although we do not go into the scope of health and wellness in this book, it is an essential part of living that cannot be ignored, and their work embraces this new business mindset.

6

The Models—Then and Now

What we have found is that the traditional business models do not seem to be working as well anymore. The way we have been doing business for the last one hundred years is based on an industrial era model. The reason these do not seem to be as effective is that things have changed; people have changed. It is now time to update our standard business models. What we see working with our Most Amazing Company models is a business model that we call the Experience Model. We will give you a brief overview in this chapter and then, in section two, go deep into how to identify and create an Experience Model. For now, let's take a quick assessment of different business models.

Traditional Hierarchy

Let's start with looking at our traditional hierarchy of an organization.

Traditional Hierarchy

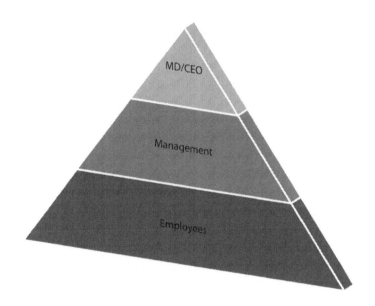

The top of the hierarchy has the full view of what is happening. Information leads to power, so it is something that is protected and coddled. This model tends to lead to a trickle-down effect of information, leaving the majority without understanding the whole picture; only their small part of it. This was necessary in the industrial age when business was compartmentalized and information was shared on a need-to-know basis. Many of our government structures still work this way. As they grow, they tend to get very process-oriented and slow in making changes.

Those days are gone. We are entering into an age of transparency which leads to turning our world upside down! But this is really a good thing once you understand how to work with it to your benefit.

The Democratic Model

This model has progressed with many forward thinking leaders.

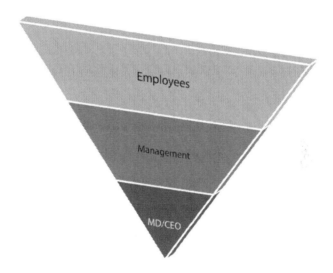

It is a model that puts the employees at the top. Since they are the ones having direct contact with the customers, they have access to more viable knowledge. There is a greater understanding of the bigger picture but is limited to within the company. The management and MD are there to support each other with the common mission and vision of the company.

> "The speed of your business is going to be the speed of the people. You can't overinvest in your people!" — *Darren Hardy, Publisher and Editorial Director of Success Magazine*

HCL Technologies, one of the leading IT Service providers in the world and one of The Most Amazing Company models, has doubled its annual revenues during the global recession because it turned its pyramid upside down and made a conscious choice to put employees first—above all else, including its customers. By doing so, they have empowered their employees to deliver best solutions and services to their customers. By putting the focus on the employees, they have actually increased their customer satisfaction and increased sales. In a very competitive market, during one of the biggest recessions, HCL has been able to not only turn around the company but also to actually position itself in a way that has made it a global leader in IT Services. By focusing on their employees through creating an environment of trust and freedom, they are showing that this model works. It is a strategy that has proven to be one of the most effective ways of transforming the way we do business.

Security comes from within

Years ago, people went to work for one company for their entire career, knowing that they had job security. The entire work environment was structured with everyone having to come to one location to do their jobs. Those days are long gone and, with the enormous amount of layoffs in the last decade, people have lost any sort of sense of security for their jobs. What they may not have realized is that job security comes from within oneself. If you are passionate about your work and bring value to the market, you can find ways to make an income from it.

On top of that, our world is changing rapidly with technology, eliminating the necessity for having to spend forty hours tied to a desk. Companies need to adapt to keeping good staff by offering flexible solutions—either in the hours or days that are required to work in the office, job sharing, and various benefits that help their employees balance their work life with their personal life.

The Shift

What we see as the shift happening in the world is a means of embracing a new way of thinking; one in which we are all connected and can contribute to the greater good of all.

This is an understanding that customers have the ability to gain as much information and knowledge in order to make informed decisions. Your customers have first contact with your front line employees—the "value" is created in that relationship. When you can turn both your employees and customers into Raving Fans, you build a solid foundation to grow exponentially. The influence and reach—the value creation—increases as we move up the inverted triangle. And the customers and partners become an integral part of the business. They are part of the success of the company.

The Shift Model

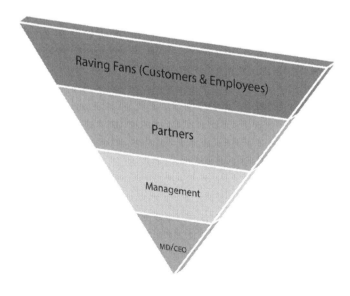

If we look at the bigger picture, a company is a system of systems within an even larger system—our world, which is the biggest ecosystem we have. What we used to view as a hierarchal structure to how everything is related is now shifting to see that we are all a part of a bigger whole. We are hearing, and understanding, more now that we are living in a networked society where we are all connected. We are interdependent on one another. Human beings and businesses have built systems that are not sustainable and have been doing considerable damage to our planet. We need to reverse this and quickly. (Whole Foods has understood this and has written a "Declaration of Interdependence".)[17]

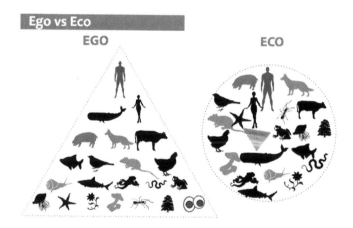

We found this image online and unfortunately do not know who to give credit to it. We added our model to show it is a part of a bigger system. It explains so much about the shift. We are understanding more and more that we are a part of an ecosystem and all that we do *does* impact the other parts. The shift is about both a "wholistic" view of the entire system and a humanistic perspective as we interact with one another.

The rigid corporate hierarchies, the industrial based thinking that is driven from the ego, are being replaced with self-organizing systems and a greater level of awareness for all living beings and our planet. Employees and customers are becoming very empowered and they are the ones driving the growth forward.

We have found that by embracing these changes, and reframing how we look at our world, our work, and our business models, we see a number of companies that are doing this in amazing ways already. And we are on a mission to find more and to help companies evolve to the next level by taking part of the quest to become Amazing Companies.

These companies are setting the standards to leaving "average" in the dust once and for all by creating and communicating their unique value to the world. They are exceeding all expectations (with their customers, employees, and partners) by being engaged and becoming Amazing Companies.

As we researched several companies that have stood out as excellent models for the rest of the world, we wanted to discover how they rise above the millions of companies that exist in the world. There are five key elements we have found that they all have in common. We call these the 5 Cultural Keys (or the 5 C's) and they are the backbone to a company:

1. **Collaboration**—an ability to work together for the greater good of all.
2. **Creativity**—innovation and a sense of continually improving.
3. **Connection**—a Thriving Culture where people are connected through shared values and purpose. There is a stronger connection to the customers.
4. **Celebration**—a focus on the achievements and an allowing to learn and grow from mistakes, and the employees have a lot of fun and give plenty of recognition.
5. **Contribution**—a clear purpose and a giving-back-to-the-world mindset.

As Jenn Lim, the cultural consultant for Zappos, says, "If you get the culture right, then the rest just falls into place."[18] Engagement revolves around the people, their passions, and the purpose. It leads to a higher productivity level; the profits are a natural result and the company is able to have a greater positive impact. We call these the 6 core elements, or our 6 P Model, which we'll discuss in more detail shortly.

The Shift also includes some other elements which we call TACT:

Transparency—You can easily Google and research anyone and find a digital footprint of their lives. (And if someone doesn't have something available, that should raise some red flags!)

Authentic—People want to do business with real people who believe in what they are doing. They want to know more about the company and make sure the values are in alignment with their own

Conscious—This is about the bigger purpose and why a company is doing what it does. Is it contributing and doing something good in the world?

Transformation—What transformation will the customer experience by using the company's product or service? There is an expectation of making the customer's life much better, or why else would they buy?

A new vocabulary is emerging because of this shift in our mindset and way of thinking. We will see more and more of this in the coming years. Our vocabulary is a reflection of our thinking and our world.

Fredrik Lindström, a Swedish linguist, comedian, film director, and speaker, says that our language is economically based right now. We use words such as value, credibility, and currency to describe more than just financial matters. New words are entering our vocabulary quickly now. For example, twenty years ago, it was unheard of to discuss meditation and mindfulness in relation to business. Now, you hear of stock brokers and financial analysts taking a break to connect and quiet their minds and top executives taking mindfulness courses to improve their wellbeing.

When we first named our company Evoloshen, we thought whether that name was too far out there or not. But only six months later, evolution and transformation were words we were hearing daily. And in the course of our interviews with employees from some of these Most Amazing Companies, the vocabulary is even more "progressive" with love, passion, contribution, collaboration, and purpose being in the forefront.

Achievers use the word love in a very smart way. To them it signifies Living Our Values Everyday. Southwest Airlines' home is Dallas Love Field, which is why they chose "LUV" as their stock ticker symbol and have infused love deep into their corporate culture. Even in Sweden, which is normally not a place where people talk about love freely, we started hearing it. GodEl's employees post pictures of themselves on Facebook holding signs that say "We Love You" for their customers. At Clarion Hotels, a division of Choice Hotels, they have a program to certify their front desk staff in caring for customers. When they have completed the class, the honor is to wear pins that say "Clarion Loves You!" That started a small movement labeling all sorts of things so that now even their coffee cups say "Clarion Loves Coffee!"

It's time to understand how each action does make an impact far greater than we were brought up to believe.

It's time to create Amazing Companies as the standard, not the exception!

The Evoloshen Program & System

We created the Evoloshen Programs and System as the bridge from our traditional business mindset to the new mindset. And we've created a way to implement The Most Amazing Company blueprint, which we will discuss later. This program is based on the high standards that we've observed with some of The Most Amazing Companies, as well as our experiences in working with small and large international companies on two continents.

We have brought in the latest trends with the gamification of work. The gaming industry probably has the most measured metrics of all industries on the planet. Data is king, and they measure things down to the nanosecond. The gamification of work is taking all the good things from the gaming industry, especially regarding engagement (minus all the killing and death), and applying it to the work world. For example, when playing an online game, you have a large goal (for example, to save the world) with many levels to pass through; all of which have challenges and opportunities to make small wins (gain a magical sword or find a shortcut). The feedback in gaming is instantaneous and often so you can correct your course as you forge on towards your mission. You work together with others and help each other to reach your goals.

Bringing these simple ideas into the work world is one of the latest trends to making work fun and engaging for employees. Our program is based on these concepts, with behavioral based activities to instill a shift in simple habits for the benefit of all. So rather than some sort of heavy change management or certification that everyone dreads, it is a light, fun, and simple way of engaging staff to take initiatives, transforming the company from the inside out.

When we work with companies, we have four phases. (You can see an infographic at www.Evoloshen.com/evoloshen-system-explained/) First we take the current status of the company through our TMAC

(The Most Amazing Company) survey. We have a workshop to get everyone on board and go through a process of selecting Amazing Ambassadors. These are the people who want to step into a leadership role and be instrumental in creating the culture and work environment with the new principles. Then we begin the Mission Possible game. We are able to drill down into the organization by implementing the elements of our system in a very fun and engaging way to create an Amazing Company that exceeds all expectations.

Phase three is the implementation and celebration phase while an organization is completing its tasks to win badges and prizes, as it accomplishes each goal and task by the working together of its employees. Once this is done, we retake the TMAC survey to see the improvements and become designated as a Most Amazing Company.

This is a system that significantly increases employee engagement in a way that will shift the mindset, increase productivity, decrease turnover and sick leave, radically improve retention, attract the best talent into the company, and overall increase the bottom line profits by at least 20 percent, if not significantly more.

We work within the framework of the 5 Cultural Keys (or the 5 C's) and the 6 core elements (AKA the 6 P's).

Many of the elements might be considered common sense, and some may seem repetitive. We integrate both the internal and external aspects of many core issues. The amazing results occur when they are integrated into a company as an entire system with the entire engagement of the company—its employees, management, and leaders. This is a collaborative method that will discover many of the answers within the organization. The program is easy to implement and has profound results on the outcome.

Yet, because each company is unique and consists of a group of people that do not exist anywhere else, it is also a system that embodies each company that works with it to achieve amazing results in its own unique way.

Join us on the journey from average, or even above average... to becoming The Most Amazing Company you've ever worked with in your life! We will show you the simple step-by-step guide you can follow in the rest of this book.

7

The Five Cultural Keys (AKA the 5 C's)

A Thriving Culture is a sound business strategy! Our model companies have put a lot of deliberate effort into fostering and nurturing a culture that is uniquely infused with their values and their employees' energy. As they grow, they work diligently to keep the core culture alive. Like we stated, there is a genuine caring for each other in the cultures of Amazing Companies.

Sometimes the cultures are so strong that they get labeled as being "cult like". We feel they are getting called that because people are *not* used to seeing large groups of employees who are so passionate about their work and love what they do. Sure, there may be some traits that could be interpreted as a cult, but as long as it is working and doing good things in the world, who cares! Let them create that Thriving Culture!

Another part of their culture is communication. Everything is transparent. All financial information is shared, so it is clear how each employee is contributing to the bottom line; recognition is given freely and the messages internally are congruent with what is being said in the market because the values and purpose are so clear. People are living their values and it shows.

Employee retention is high, as people feel they are not working, but rather playing with their friends and family. Attracting top talent becomes quite easy because they have Raving Fans of their employees and their customers. People are drawn to the positive, fun energy of these companies and, often, they have more than hundreds, even thousands, of applicants applying than they have openings available. This makes it possible for them to bring the best person on board for each position, which obviously helps in maintaining their growth momentum. The culture is probably the most important key to their success and they know it. So they work very actively to create, maintain, and nurture their culture.

Zappos has become quite a popular example for how they have developed their culture and are known for some of their zaniness. TOMS Shoes culture seeps out into the customer base, as they share a strong bond of knowing they are helping children and people in need and making their lives just a little bit better in such a simple way with a pair of shoes or a pair of glasses. Southwest Airlines is known as one of the most fun airlines, where everyone chips in to give their customers a great experience. Whole Foods is filling a growing demand for healthy food with a company motto stating "Whole Foods, Whole People, Whole Planet" and a great example of bringing together and empowering people for the greater good of all.

Culture is like the air we breathe. We can't see it, but we know it's there keeping us alive. It is an intangible part of a company, which we haven't necessarily figured out fully how to measure... but it is the fabric that weaves the values, mission, passions, and purpose together in any company.

> "Everything that can be *counted* does not necessarily *count*; everything that *counts* cannot necessarily be *counted*.
> — *Albert Einstein*

The 5 Cultural Keys are what we consider the umbrella, the overlying principles, that The Most Amazing Companies all have in common. There is a definite energy and vibrancy in these companies, and we believe they are doing well because their focus, whether deliberate or accidental, has shifted from the norm. They have embraced these five keys and infused it into the soul of the company.

1. **Collaboration**

   This is going *way* beyond teamwork. We see it as a much deeper connection and a genuine caring of the employees. Employees take a vested interest in each other and understand that a group working together elevates everyone. Therefore, it is easy to give and support one another. The whole is stronger than its separate parts.

   Employees tend to become good friends in Amazing Companies. They are there for each other beyond the 8-5 work hours. They tend to bond by spending time together after hours, on the weekends, and on trips. They fall in love with each other, get married, and their children also become friends. They also go to weddings and celebrate birthdays and big events.

   Even in the market, we see competition as the old mindset. Collaboration is taking over. Stronger value connections are forming with customers, as loyalty increases and customer evangelists want to see the success of the company. So-called competitors are sharing the market because they understand that they are there to serve their customers and the market and do not have fear that they will lose business by doing so. Quite the contrary, they know that by sharing messages, the *right* customers will be attracted to them at the *right* time, so there is no threat to collaborate with other companies in their market. They also form stronger relationships with the suppliers and vendors—and treat them as friends and good business partners—by taking a personal interest in them as well.

It's been shown time after time that when people work together in a collaborative environment, they achieve more than if there is a competitive driving force that is pitting them against each other. The new paradigm shift is about supporting and giving back.

Amazing Companies know that a collaborative business works well—it exists for the good of everyone. There is a definite energy that comes from employees who enjoy working together. This extends outwards beyond the walls of the company to their partners, affiliates, suppliers, and vendors, as relationships are treated with respect and caring for each other.

2. **Creativity**

   Amazing Companies allow creativity to flourish and they encourage it wholeheartedly. Some of the best ideas have come from deep within the company as we'll share examples of this in this book. Innovation is held high, freedom and trust allow for employees to tap into their creative forces for the good of the company—and it shows.

   When employees are allowed and encouraged to be creative, a company taps into huge resources that can make a huge difference in the company and its impact. It opens the flow for people to tap into their full potential, which, in turn, creates excited, motivated, and engaged employees. Productivity increases when someone feels they have the ability to expand and grow to reach their highest potential. Industries do vary on the levels of creativity as well as the type of environment—an ad agency has a very different culture from a steel mill.

We believe that each and every person has a gift and a purpose they, and only they, can bring into the world. It might sound a bit fluffy... but it *is* true. Each individual is unique in his or her own ways. **The exact person you are—born to specific parents on a specific date and time—with the DNA structure you have has about a 1:400,000,000,000,000 (that's one in 400 trillion!) chance of existing![19]**

We should be celebrating our uniqueness because it is truly miraculous!

> "There are two ways to live: You can live as if nothing is a miracle; you can live as if everything is a miracle." —*Albert Einstein*

It is interesting that someone with such a great scientific mind as Albert Einstein would talk about life in such an esoteric way. And just as each person is unique... so is each company! Products and services can be copied easily, but the culture of a company cannot. Allowing each employee to shine with their gift—which means making sure they are well matched to their work so that they are truly passionate about it—brings a surge of creative energy into an organization.

Creativity doesn't mean it needs to be way out there; depending on the culture, some guidelines are necessary. Allowing the employees to feel that they can come with new ideas and create an environment where they can think outside of the box is good for both the people and the company.

3. Connection

We are connected in so many ways. A Thriving Culture is where people are connected through shared values and a common purpose. Amazing companies have mastered connecting with people, both internally with their employees and externally with their customers and partners. When a group of people come together because of what they believe in, they are connected on a much deeper level and will support each other more for the greater purpose.

When you feel a connection with someone, you care about them, you feel more compassion and understanding toward them, and you are drawn to them. You have a heightened sense of awareness because of the connection you feel. The same thing happens on an organizational level. People are attracted to work for a company where they feel that very same connection. And people stay longer when that connection is strong.

Technology has connected us on a global basis in incredible ways. It is showing us that our actions really do matter. Ericsson, a global Swedish telecom company, talks about a "networked society" and how, as technology advances, everything will be connected.

We have believed that we were not connected to others, that our actions were isolated and only had a limited impact. It has become evident that this is not the case. Let's take honeybees as an example. They are small insects, so you might think it wouldn't really matter if a few of them died off because of pesticides, right? We are discovering that it does make a huge difference. Those bees are responsible for pollination and, without that, our entire food chain is being disrupted. We are *all* connected in ways that we are just beginning to fathom.

It is a safer bet to understand that our actions really do make a difference. This is why it is so important to be very aware of the consequences that can happen because of those actions. Because companies are groups of people working together for a shared purpose, it is important to understand the full implications of connection and use it as a force for good; to make a positive impact in all that they do.

4. **Celebration**

Who doesn't need more fun in their lives? This is by far the one key that seems to be the toughest for most companies to master. We all take ourselves so seriously. We need to lighten up! We seem to have forgotten somewhere along the road to growing up our childlike nature with curiosity and the ability to laugh often.

Did you know the average 4 year-old laughs 300 times a day and for the average 40 year-old it might be 4 times?[20] We also tend to be so focused on reaching goals, which is a good thing, except that we forget to enjoy the journey. We've created a societal belief that we need to work hard to achieve our goals and then we'll have fun. Somewhere along the line, the fun diminishes more and more as each year passes.

Amazing Companies are bringing the fun back into work and reminding us to still keep our childlike nature alive and well. The environment and physical offices tend to be bright and full of color. Some companies even look like big playgrounds! And they take the time to do fun things together. They joke around, play tricks on each other, and have mascots and rituals that keep the culture alive and well. And, despite so, they seem to have super productive employees too, so it isn't all fun and games all the time either. They get results and are reaching their objectives.

Recognition and appreciation abound as everyone tends to let others know what a good job they've done.

Achievements are rewarded and honored publicly. Achievers know this and have built an entire company around just this idea. Research shows that 64 percent of people leaving their jobs do so because they do not feel appreciated. Disengaged employees cost companies $300 billion per year in lost productivity! A simple action as acknowledging a job well done and giving recognition makes an employee more motivated to deliver superior work and customer service, which, in turn, increases customer loyalty and leads to better business results.[21]

Mistakes are celebrated as a learning experience to grow from, alleviating a lot of the stress and fear of failure that can be paralyzing for some. There is a well known story about a young management trainee that had recently started with IBM. He was quite ambitious and ended up making a costly mistake that cost the company over $1 million. When the CEO asked to see him, the trainee was certain that was the end of his short-lived career at IBM. Shaking, pale, and fully prepared to receive the chewing out of his lifetime along with his notice, the CEO stunned him by saying that now they had invested so much into this young fellow's learning, that he had better stick around and prove he was worth it.

A fun work environment helps creativity, strengthens relationships, and brings positive energy into the workplace. Amazing Companies know that having fun makes people happier, so it makes them enjoy their jobs. It increases employee wellbeing and productivity, reduces sick leave and employee turnover, and makes recruitment easier. All this leads to a more profitable company.

MindValley has annual F.A.D. (Female Appreciation Days) and M.A.D. (Male Appreciation Days), where they celebrate each other and the wonderful differences that bring diversity and creativity into their culture.

Southwest Airlines knows that flying can be very stressful for their customers, so they use humor as a way to help people relax. Anyone who has ever experienced one of their flights has probably laughed a few times during the flight. They are known for their announcements[22] that will make even the most serious person break out in a belly laugh:

- "Everyone on the plane's left side, toward the terminal, put your faces in the window and smile, so our competitors can see what a full flight looks like."
- "In the unlikely event of a cabin depressurization, please secure your mask and then decide which child you like better."
- "Please be careful when retrieving your luggage and personal belongings from the overhead bins. Shift happens."
- "We got you here roughly 25 minutes early. So next time you fly Southwest and we happen to be running late, remember that you owe us 25 minutes."
- "This is a no complaining, no whining, no smoking flight. If you absolutely must smoke, I suggest you avail yourself of our smoking area out on the wing... that is, if you can manage to get it lit. While you're out there, feel free to enjoy our in-flight movie, *Gone with the Wind*."
- "We don't expect a loss of cabin pressure today. If we did, the three of us would have called in sick. But if we do lose pressure, masks will automatically fall from the ceiling. After you're done screaming, simply put the mask on and breathe normally."

We could continue for quite some time, but you get the idea. Celebration includes fun, laughter, recognition, appreciation, and ability to make mistakes and learn from them. It also includes having an environment where employees enjoy working together and where customers feel a sense of joy in their interactions with the company.

5. **Contribution**

Finally, the key of giving back. Contribution is a critical key to creating that bigger purpose that will drive a business forward by leaps and bounds. It doesn't matter if the contribution is on a local community level or in tackling some of our global problems like hunger and environmental issues. The business has a purpose that is clearly defined, the values are infused into the organization through its people, and the element of giving is what motivates employees to do their best.

Even doing boring work, like filling out an excel sheet and crunching numbers (well, ok that might be exciting for some still), becomes significant and meaningful when the employee knows that he or she is contributing to making the world a better place in some way. They stop being a cog in the machine and know that what they do makes a difference—they are able to contribute on a personal level to a company contributing on a much bigger level. This excites them to get up in the morning and come to work.

There is a Universal Law of giving that companies have discovered that works well in business. When you give freely without expectations or attachments, you will receive, often even greater in value, and not necessarily from the same source. In other words, give value to your customers and potential customers, and you will attract even more to your business. When a company has giving ingrained into the DNA of the company—such as TOMS, Whole Foods, and Virgin—the company will grow exponentially in ways that may even be unexpected.

TOMS' One-For-One Movement shows how the contributive model gives back in ways that founder Blake Mycoskie couldn't even imagine when he founded the company. In his book, *Build Something That Matters,* he shares the story of his first giving trip. Putting shoes on children's feet and seeing their eyes aglow with delight changed him forever, and he knew he'd found his life's work—his calling. It was such a profound shift in how he viewed the world. When so many people had told him his idea would never work, it was proof that you could build a company with a mission to touch lives significantly and make a profit at the same time.

When the employees are excited, driven, passionate, and highly productive at work, this energy will spread within a company and propel the whole business forward. It is the core of the business, the soul of the company, and it is not possible to exist without the people working there. Contribution is what brings significance and meaning back into the workplace and makes the Age of Transformation possible.

We'll be exploring how many of these Amazing Companies are doing business differently and how they are thriving and engaged. These keys are woven throughout the fabric of their being. The clues and signs are everywhere and, even if not clearly stated, it is clearly lived and experienced within their DNA.

Leaders of all companies have a choice now. The choice is to try to hold onto the status quo... or to embrace a new mindset and an empowering way of doing business. Employees are the heart and soul of a company. You take care of them and the company will thrive and grow. Give them the opportunity to be the best that they can be and watch to see just how much the company will transform. It is, after all, the Age of Transformation. We're evolving... and this is a very good thing!

Besides the 5 C's that are essential to creating an Amazing Company, we have identified 6 core elements that impact a company. They all start with *P* so we call them the 6 P's. (Isn't that convenient? The 5 C's and the 6 P's—that's easy enough to remember, right?) They are Purpose, Passion, People, Productivity, Profits, and Positive Impact. We believe very strongly in doing our internal work—that inner homework—on an individual basis *and* on an organizational level as well. The first three P's are internally focused, while the next three are external results that come from doing the first three. That is why we have them in this order.

Now let's explore the six core elements and show how these Amazing Companies are making a difference in the world.

Section Two

Creating The Most Amazing Company Your Step by Step Guide

The 6 Core Elements (AKA the 6 P's)

8

Purpose

The first core element is the purpose. It is essential to know why you do what you do. Whether it is for the organization or the individual, this is the North Star, the guiding light that leads you on the right path. A company exists to bring value into the world and, as it grows, it becomes a living entity in itself. It is the sum of all the people involved. The purpose must be clear and communicated to everyone in a way that is understood so that everyone is on the same boat, so to speak.

This is one of the key foundational elements that you can build your company on... and your life too. When a company is not in touch with its purpose, it will be lost. It will not be communicating in a way that will reach its full potential and certainly not from a place of values that will attract the ideal customers and top talents.

Most companies do have their vision and mission statement well versed. The question is: Is it coming from the heart and soul of the company? Do the employees know it and base their decisions daily from this perspective? When the purpose (why you do what you do) is aligned with the values of the culture and the people, then things start to become crystal-clear and decisions become much easier to make for anyone within the company. A company may have a purpose well defined, but the important question to ask is: is it a purpose that will inspire others to take action? If not, it is probably not the bigger purpose. We can lift a company's purpose to a much higher level just by asking "and why do we do that?" several times until you discover that higher purpose for being.

When anyone does this exercise on a personal level, eventually we end up with just a few core reasons: love, happiness, and peace. Before you write this off as just metaphysical mumbo jumbo, try it out yourself. Why do you do what you do? Let's say you're an executive of a company. You want to make a good living. Why is that? Because you want to live a good life and take care of your family. Why is that? Because you want to make them happy. Why is that? Because it'll make you feel good. Why is that? Because you want to be happy too. It's a simple exercise and it shows that even though we all come from different walks of life, we all have the same core desires within us... which doesn't make us so different from each other after all.

In the following section, we will be exploring the importance of the Why Formula, having Aligned Values, and the Bigger Purpose. Like building a house and putting down a strong foundation, this is the first foundation block to creating an Amazing Company.

1. The Why Formula

> "Get clear on the reason why you're doing what it is that you're doing because if the why is big enough, the how is easy."
> — *Darren Hardy, editor and founder of Success Magazine*

■ Why do you do what you do?

A simple question... but a much more profound one than it first appears to be. Knowing the answer to this is going to be your guiding light to everything that you do. Cars are not selling cars; they are selling safety or luxury or some sort of experience the customer wants. A company making locks isn't selling just locks; they are selling security and peace of mind. Figure out the real reason behind why you are doing what you are doing—both on a personal level and within the company. And then find ways to elevate it to an even higher level.

■ The big picture and purpose

Each person has unique talents and strengths. No other person in the world has the same combination. The same is true for a company. It is a unique group of people coming together to create value in some way.

Knowing the purpose and being able to communicate it clearly to the market will help in positioning your company in a way that makes it unique. When you have a higher purpose as to why you are doing what you do, you'll attract more customers and employees to your company more easily.

If your purpose is only to make money, or add shareholder value, it is not sustainable. People these days want to be associated with companies that are really making a positive difference in the world.

> "Your company exists not to make money. Your company exists to advance something, to do something more—and it should be for other human beings." —*Simon Sinek*

A company is a system, just as an individual, a family, and even the Universe. When you know how to optimize the system, you bring the best into your world. A big part of this is in knowing why you exist. In the business world, it is the reason why the company exists. Here are a few examples from our model companies:

- TOMS Shoes—it is a one-to-one movement; not a shoe.
- Zappos—it is all about customer service and the customer experience, and the company breaths this through each and every employee and through every action each employee takes.
- MindValley—it is about optimizing human potential through personal development products and education.
- Virgin—their brand is all about taking on the status quo, having a really fun time doing it, and using business as a force for good.
- HCL Technologies—putting employees first has taken this global technology company to $4 billion in revenues in 3 years—and the primary focus has shifted to their people.
- Whole Foods—they know that whole foods make whole people, which makes for a whole planet.
- Southwest—has three passions: "our performance, our people, and our planet", and they LUV their customers.
- Achievers—changing the way the world works through recognition.

Sense of purpose—Why does the company exist, what does it stand for? What are you resolved to accomplish? What is the obsessive focus, the "true North", that drives all company behavior? Why was the business started in the first place? Did it spring from a passion for a certain activity, like camping or metalworking? Was it started to fill a perceived need in the marketplace?

What is the ultimate reason for your business?

Your purpose, your why, is your unique offering

It is your reason for being. It is the source fueling your vision.

On a personal level, your purpose answers the question "Why am I here?" It is your North Star—the bright light, which guides and directs you as you adventure through life. When you make conscious choices grounded in your essence of who you really are, you discover and refine your purpose.

Ask yourself the following questions:

- What do I stand for at my best?
- What is my unique contribution in the world?
- And look to your past for clues. If you string together the defining moments of your life, they will often point to a theme or a definite calling.
- Follow that thread. You may discover your purpose at a young age, it may come to you in a flash moment in your life, or, most commonly, your purpose may continually evolve as you do.

Doing the work for yourself, as well as defining the bigger purpose for your company, is part of the evolution and the journey you are in.

■ Partnership

Working in partnership is important because it takes us away from the "us vs. them" mindset and brings us to the "we" mindset. We are working together for a greater purpose. Employees feel important because they see the bigger picture and feel they are an integral part of that process.

In *Tribal Leadership* by Dave Logan, John King, and Halee Fischer-Wright, they discuss the difference between working with dyads (two people) versus triads (three people). As long as the goals and purpose are clear and everyone is in agreement, the teams working with three are able to accomplish more by each individual working less.

> The whole is more than the sum of its parts.
> — *Aristotle, Metaphysica*

This concept has been around for ages, but it can be difficult to implement when the individuals are working on their own agenda. When the purpose and values are aligned both professionally and personally, the productivity and results will skyrocket!

■ The Message

It is critical that the purpose is conveyed in *all* communications, both internally and externally. Marketing, branding, and communication play a vital role in making sure that the Bigger Purpose is understood. Their focus must also be with internal marketing and communication as well. Their Raving Fans exist in both places!

There is a shift happening in terms of understanding your market. Instead of focusing on demographics and traditional marketing means, an emerging trend is to look at the market from a *values* perspective. And excellent resource for a deeper understanding of the shift in humanity is the book *The Cultural Creatives: How 50 Million People Are Changing the World,* by sociologist Paul H. Ray and psychologist Sherry Ruth Anderson, which was first published in 2000. In it, they describe an emerging market segment that they call Cultural Creatives. They discuss the differences between Traditionalists, Modernists, and the Cultural Creatives. A very brief summary of each is:

Traditionalists: do not embrace change. Old school thinking. Industrial age. Conservative politics. Religious beliefs. Tend to be older white men. Live in fear-based thinking. This market segment is shrinking rapidly as they are literally dying off.

Modernists: believe in financial materialism. Not on the religious right. Not self-actualizing. Not idealistic. Secular. Tend to believe nature is sacred. Have orthodox religion and beliefs. Success is a high priority. Tend to be logical, analytical, and reasonable. Want things to make sense to them. Curious about how things work.

Cultural Creatives (CC's): like to travel. See nature as sacred. Have general green values. View relationships as important. Success is not a high priority (it's more about impact and contribution). Pro feminism in work place. Not concerned about own job. Interested in self-actualization. Don't believe in financial materialism. Want to be activists. Although their focus is not on material wealth, they don't have financial problems. Believe in humanistic psychology. Have optimism about the future. Want creative time.

It is estimated that in five to ten years the CC's could be over half of the American population, and the numbers have grown significantly throughout Europe. There are literally hundreds of millions of CC's across the globe, yet what is interesting about this is that they feel they are alone. This is the fastest growing market segment globally but because they are not talking openly about their view points and values to each other, they often feel isolated. Frigyes Fogel is the producer and director of the Cultural Creatives—The (R)evolution movie that explains and highlights some of the great work being done and companies run by CC's. (You can find this excellent film at www.CulturalCreatives.CC.)

Traditionalists are declining constantly and Modernists are often recruited into CC segments. As times passes, Modernists tend to go to CC activities and self-actualization becomes a priority. For example, in the 1970s yoga and meditation was considered "woowoo"; now it is totally incorporated in the norms of the Modernist segment.

Understanding how society and the world are changing rapidly is essential in how we communicate with everyone. We've gone from the Industrial Age to the Information Age. We believe we have already passed the Information Age now and have entered into the Transformation Age—a time when people want purpose and meaning in their lives. Technology is speeding up not only our lives but also our access to evolution, and each shift is happening in shorter and shorter intervals of time... to the extent that we've already experienced several "Ages" within our lifetime already!

It's time to change our mindset, the way we are educated, and the way we do business! *That* is what will make or break companies going into the future. Those that can adapt and evolve will not only survive; they will thrive. And those that do not will disappear as they are made completely obsolete.

Take the example of Kodak, a company that was founded in 1888 and held dominant position in photographic film throughout the twentieth century, reaching upwards of 90 percent of the market in the 1980s. But a technological disruption occurred with the invention of digital photography. This caused the downfall of this long-standing global brand. In the 1990s, Kodak was slow in transition to the digital photography market and went into a downward spiral in their business during the first decade of the new millennium. As of this writing, they will be emerging from bankruptcy courts in 2013, and only time will tell if they will be able to reinvent themselves and make a comeback.

Companies must be evolving in order to stay in the game. Do you want to be a dinosaur... or a transformative force in the world?

2. Aligned Values

Zappos is a Most Amazing Company that is a driving force in changing the face of customer service, customer experience, and company culture. They are innovative and changing the way we do business by becoming a stellar example that others can model.

One of the ways they have accomplished this is by becoming very clear on their values... and defining them within the organization so that each and every person can not only follow these values at work but to live their lives by them as well! Their values are not just lip service coming from the top down. They are values that are a part of who they are and how they are choosing to live their lives. This connects—and engages—the employees to the company on a much deeper level and helps the employees to make solid decisions. This also makes it much easier to recruit the right people to the organization.

**Clearly defined values that are aligned are
like a North Star guiding them to their destination**

How many companies out there have defined values but none of the employees know what they are? In our experience, the vast majority of the companies have taken steps to define values... but the problem is that they have come from the top down—the leaders have defined them; not the employees. This is why most employees don't really care about the values and this leads to disengagement in the company.

Zappos defined their core values from within the organization. They brainstormed a list, narrowed it down to 37, emailed it to the entire company, and narrowed it down to the top 10 that the employees voted on. As Tony Heish, the CEO of Zappos, says in his book, *Delivering Happiness,*[23] about creating values:

- When created from inside the company, they stand true to the company.
- No two cultures are exactly alike, yet company values often sound the same.
- Need to be unique to your company.
- Becomes a natural part of employees' everyday language and way of thinking.
- Integrated into a company's operations and align an entire organization.
- Serves as a guide for employees to make their own decisions.
- Core values are essentially a formalized definition of a company's culture.
- Your personal core values define who you are, and a company's core values ultimately define the company's character and brand.
- For individuals, character is destiny.
- For organizations, culture is destiny.

Here are the core values that Zappos is living and working by:

❶ Deliver WOW through service.

❷ Embrace & drive change.

❸ Create Fun & a Little Weirdness.

❹ Be adventurous, creative, & open-minded.

❺ Pursue growth & Learning.

❻ Build open & honest relationships with communication.

❼ Build a positive team & Family Spirit.

❽ Do More With Less.

❾ Be passionate & determined.

❿ Be Humble.

Determining values is a process that generally should take some time. Do not rush because it is such an essential part of defining the entire company culture and outlook. Once you have a list of core values that are in alignment with what you want to accomplish, and that everyone can live by, the company culture begins to shift dramatically.

■ Create a clear value system

The answers to this objective lie within the organization. This is something that needs to be developed and fostered from inside. The values won't mean anything unless they come from within. When they come from the employees, then they will buy into the value system and make it a living, breathing part of the organization.

Even if the values end up being the same or similar, it is essential that this exercise goes out into the organization. When the employees feel that their opinions are important, and listened to, they will have a much greater feeling of contribution to the organization. They will feel empowered and valued, therefore it is of vital importance that they are able to give their answers and vote on what they think fit in best. The leaders and team responsible for this exercise will have the final say, but with the input from the organization, it makes this a very powerful and connecting foundational block to creating an Amazing Company.

■ Have values that you can live by in life too

> "A wide gap between business and human values can reduce the life expectancy of companies." — *Firms of Endearment*

When the values come from within, it becomes such a natural way of being. Every decision is made in alignment with the values of the company. When people can live their lives by these values as well, then they don't need to think about them. PUMA, for example, keeps it very simple. They have four core values that are easy to live by: Fair, Honest, Positive, and Creative.

Zappos created a culture book that included their top 10 values that they run their business by so that each and every employee knows, understands, and easily lives his or her life from this foundation. And they have been very generous—meaning very transparent—in sharing this with the world as well to the benefit of us all.

We spend almost a third of our adult lives at work. The separation between work and personal lives is getting harder and harder to distinguish because of the connectivity of the world these days. Who can turn off their cell phones, not check their emails, or get online for more than a couple of days? Who doesn't sleep with their cell phone next to them?

As we mentioned earlier, Achievers, another of our model companies, talks about creating a culture of L.O.V.E. at work. This is an acronym for Living Our Values Everyday. Their website communicates these values very clearly: "Our values are the foundation for everything we do. They help us create great work, build team spirit, and stay focused on the bottom line. Plus, we have a lot of fun sharing the L.O.V.E with our coworkers and customers." You can see that these are values that make sense and are easy to live by. This brings cohesiveness to the organization on a deep level and brings a sense of shared connection that cannot be created any other way.

Achievers Values

Focus on Customer Happiness
We all have a "Customer", whether internal or external. We'll stop at nothing to do what it takes to make them happy and successful.

Care, Share & Be Fair
Be thoughtful and helpful to those around you. Be generous with your knowledge and time. Treat others with respect and when in doubt, always take the high road.

Live Passionately
Enthusiasm is contagious. Spread your excitement to those around you.

Embrace R&D & Innovation
Stand on the shoulders of giants and then take it to the next level. Don't reinvent the wheel.

Embrace Real-Time Communication
Have open, honest and timely conversations. Solicit feedback; it will only make you better.

Act with a Sense of Ownership
We are all owners of Achievers and are accountable for doing what we commit to. We'll do whatever it takes to succeed.

Build a Positive Team Spirit
Business is a team sport. Your positive attitude will help overcome the challenges of building a great company.

Learn from Failure & Celebrate Success
Sometimes you win, sometimes you learn. Failures is not the opposite of success; it is on the road to it. Fail fast, improve and you ultimately persevere.

■ Recruit people who have the same values

You attract and hire the best people for your organization based on their values. This will be a big part of them staying longer with the company. In our headhunting days, we've always matched personality to culture—first and foremost—because the job and the skills can easily change. If someone is to stay longer with a company, they need to fit into the environment and culture, and a big part of developing a particular culture is in the values of the company and the people working there.

For example, if someone doesn't smoke and believes that it is harmful for an individual, then they would never feel comfortable working for a tobacco company, regardless of how perfect the job was or how great the pay was. If you match someone with their belief system, they are going to go beyond your expectations just because they have a passion for the company and what they are doing.

Someone who wants to change the world isn't going to work for a company that is "old school" or, if they do, they may get too frustrated and eventually leave. All too often, we've seen individuals who made a job change, thinking the company was a certain way only to discover to their dismay that it isn't at all the same as they thought. The level of disappointment is high and the person feels either stuck or desperate to leave. It is critical to get a strong match with the values so that you can have happy and engaged employees delivering excellent results.

3. The Bigger Purpose

The Bigger Purpose is a clear definition of why the company exists. When we explore this with companies, we always find a deeper reason that very often is *not* communicated out into the organization or the market.

Your company's mission statement is your purpose in action. It is how you express your purpose through what you do. And personally, you live your mission by expressing your essence consistently through the choices you make.

What is a bigger purpose? Simply put, it's a definitive statement about the difference that you are trying to make in the world. Organizations, leaders, and brands with a real and genuine purpose are primed to deliver success not only in the marketplace but also where it really counts—in the lives of others.

There *is* a bigger purpose for an organization. And when it's crystal-clear to the market, then the company grows exponentially.

■ Changing the rules of the game

When the purpose for existing becomes big enough, there is no competition! You can change the rules of the game by lifting the purpose of existence to new heights. When you change the rules of the game, you then can invite others to play with you.

A great example of this is something MindValley did. This Internet based company that delivers personal development products and services has discovered ways of creating beautiful web pages that convert sales at a much higher rate that what has been the industry "norm". They decided to share all the things they are doing inside of the company (again we come back to transparency) to help other companies create better websites because they know that consumers want to have a great experience online. They openly share all their design and sales conversion strategies. By doing this, they are setting the standards even higher for everyone else. They are improving the global online presence. And by doing this, who is setting the standards? They are, of course. It's their game. But it's not being done just for the sake of winning the game, because they know that if everyone plays this game, everyone will win. There is a greater purpose for it.

■ Give meaning to all you do—it's your calling

> The two greatest days in your life are the day you were born... and the day you find out why. — *Mark Twain*

Every single person on this planet has a reason for being here. It's up to each person to discover what that reason is—or not, if they choose not to. And every company has a purpose. When the purpose becomes greater than the sum of its parts, that is when greatness can emerge. When the purpose is clearly defined, decision making becomes much easier—either you do it for the good of the company or you don't. Is it in alignment with where the company wants to go? When you have significance in what you do, it makes it worthwhile to spend your time doing it.

If you were given $84,600 dollars per day and you had to spend them all in one day, what would you do? If you go to our YouTube channel, you'll find a video about the value of time. www.youtube.com/voloshen

Time is the great equalizer. Every person on this planet has only 24 hours—or 84,600 seconds—in a day. How are you investing that time? When the employees know their own purpose, the organization can move on towards reaching its purpose through the maximization of the productivity of the group.

■ Team dynamics (get rid of the "us" and "them", it's a "we" mentality)

When you have collaboration with a higher purpose in the forefront, you shift from an "us vs. them mentality" to a "we mentality". It stops being about *me* and focuses on *we*. Having a common goal and a higher purpose gives clarity, eliminates competition, and gets people working together to find the best solutions to whatever the challenge or problem might be. That bigger purpose lifts the group up from small minded thinking and begins to remove the pettiness that can often be present in a group dynamic.

In some companies, often in bigger organizations, there tends to be a lot of office politics, gossiping, scheming, backstabbing, and other destructive behaviors that are counter-productive for everyone. Sometimes the management is very authoritative, demanding, and micromanaging, which takes away the ability for someone to flourish in their own creativity. All of these negative environments negatively affect the individuals working there.

The question is, do you *really* want to be in an environment where people are afraid, just hanging on to get their paychecks, and are walking on eggshells because they don't want to get into trouble? Or do you want to be in an environment where people absolutely love what they are doing, are supportive of each other, and are creative and improving the entire organization? Who wants to live in a dictatorship? Clearly we've seen that model doesn't work—so why would it be any good in the work place?

Creating an environment where everyone is working together in a supportive and positive way is good for everyone! When the bigger purpose is clearly defined, communicated, and is an integral part of why every action is taken, the company will have an entirely different energy within. This will pull the teams together to each excel in their part of the bigger picture. It is much easier when they know what that is and see the importance to what they are doing each day.

It is possible to create a "zone of amazingness" not only internally within the organization but also externally in the market place. It comes down to knowing the bigger purpose and positioning the company in a place that eliminates all competition because the purpose is one that everyone can support and root for in the world.

TOMS Shoes has trailblazed the one-for-one business model by donating shoes for each pair sold. They have created a niche for themselves that no one can compete with because their bigger purpose is to provide safety and health for children in need. They have created a zone of amazingness that motivates their employees and customers to new levels of commitment and dedication.

I:CO, or I:Collect, a Swiss based recycling company is on a mission to create a closed loop recycling solution in the textile industry. That means that all unwanted clothing and shoes can be brought to their partner stores and locations for store credits. They coordinate with logistics companies using a reverse logistics strategy to make their businesses more efficient and productive to pick up in locations they are already delivering packages. Then they take the used clothing and shoes and distribute it through their system to either reuse, repurpose, or recycle. Their purpose is to support the textile industry to create systems that are fully sustainable that are good for the people and the planet. Because they are looking at all levels in the process from consumers and manufacturers to distribution and recycling, they are an excellent model of collaboration with a higher purpose.

A small Australian start-up company that has a passion for helping a big issue of waste management in developing countries took this bigger purpose to a whole new level. Three engineers saw a big need in developing countries and wanted to do something about it. The way they looked at it, everyone needs to have toilet paper and it is a product in constant demand. Why not link that to helping others? Their business model is giving 50 percent of the profits of their toilet paper—called "Who Gives A Crap?"—to Water Aid, which is helping with sanitation issues in many countries. Then to launch the start of their company and seek capital to get started, they choose to do a tongue-and-cheek campaign to raise $50,000 through a popular social fundraising site. One of the founders, Simon Griffiths, decided to sit on the toilet until they reached their goal and they made a very funny video. Luckily for Simon, this video went viral and he only needed to stay positioned there fifty hours before they raised their $50,000 goal.[24]

We share this example to show that you can create a bigger purpose for anything! Most companies will not need to take such extreme measures—but it certainly did capture the attention they wanted for their cause.

Social entrepreneurism is a clear movement of tapping into that bigger purpose to make a positive difference in the world. There is no denying that the companies that will thrive in the future will have their bigger purpose at the forefront of all that they do.

And it makes sense because it's just a good way to do business.

9

Passion

Passion is really the heart of all that we do. It is what motivates us, drives us, and gives us the energy and excitement to accomplish what we set out to do. Without the fires of passion burning within, a person loses momentum, enthusiasm, and motivation. Things become lackluster. Think about when you've fallen in love in your life or the first time you held your newborn child in your arms. The colors looked brighter, the sounds were clearer, and it felt like your heart was going to burst with love and joy. (Hopefully you've had this experience in your life at some point so you know what we are talking about!)

It *is* possible to bring that kind of energy into our work too. When we know what we are passionate about, only then we can reach our full potential. If you think about the words job and passion, which one would you rather spend your time on? A job has become synonymous with drudgery, a drag; something you *have—not want—*to do, and it drains your energy. Whereas having a passion for your work is energizing, something you are looking forward to, that you cannot wait to dive into to, and it makes you happy.

Hire people for their passions. Do not offer jobs anymore but rather an opportunity to fulfill a passion. HCL's Anand Pillai, a senior vice president, sums up the intent well: "Find the job you love and you'll never have to work a day in your life."[25]   Part of HCL's culture transformation included eliminating employee satisfaction surveys and instead initiate a survey measuring the employees passions called EPIC (which stands for Employee Passion Indicative Count).[26]

When passion is strong and it is identified and understood, it is possible to harness that energy to create great things and have a big impact in the world. This is true on all levels of our world— individual, family, company, national and world (although we have yet to reach this ideal so far). Passions are expansive, creative, and drive you to make progress.

Martin Luther King Jr. and Mahatma Ghandi are two examples of leaders who made a huge impact because of their passion to make the world a better place. If you look at any successful company, the founders tend to be great leaders who had both passion and vision.

Tapping into the power of passion is essential to being able to accomplish what you want with yourself and with your company. Getting others to feel that same passion and add their personal passions is what energizes a group of people to greatness.

Everything is energy. Understanding how to use the personal energy of yourself and the people in your "circle of influence", whether that is your employees, coworkers, management teams, family members, community groups, governments, etc., is what will propel you further and further towards your goals and dreams.

Passion is when the fires within ignite. Passion in work turns it into play, something that you love to do. It is the unseen power of any organization and truly inspiring leaders know how to tap into it.

Tony Collins, CEO of Virgin Trains, discovered the passion of his people in a very traditional industry. He stated in a speech:

> *"What is remarkable about our experience in trains is how the same people who delivered the service under British Rail and were seen to be largely cold and disinterested toward the passengers are the same people who now deliver industry leading customer service, so the passion was always there. It had been suppressed, devalued, destroyed by a command and control structure driven by process, status and fear. All we had to do was release it."[27]*

Organizational energy is created from the collective energy of the group. It is released when the people are "emotionally and intellectually excited by the firm's vision and values."[28] Passion is a much more powerful energy than that fear, dread, or boredom. What overall organizational energy do you have in your company right now?

Passion is what creates an enthusiastic environment, where anything can be possible and the only limits come from small thinking. Donald Trump is known for saying if you're going to think, you may as well think big. It's that big thinking that comes from being passionate. Here we will look at how the WOW factor differentiates you from others, why having Full Engagement of employees is critical, and how to reach the state of Flow.

Do not underestimate the power of passion.
Passionate people are your strongest asset.

1. The WOW Factor

■ The unique experience

What is the WOW factor of your company? What we mean by the WOW factor is that there is something so special about you and what you do that your customers, employees, and partners choose to work with you because they cannot get this anywhere else.

Amazing Companies are excelling and outstanding at what they do—they have a WOW factor. They work on this. Whether it is consciously developed or not, they have it.

The good news is that if you do not currently have a WOW factor, you can develop it and really find a way to differentiate yourself from everyone else out there. When you do this, you've suddenly stepped out of the whole competition model of doing business. (We'll get more into this later.)

A WOW factor is something that makes the person experiencing your product or service or employment say "WOW! I just love this!" And isn't that what we want all of our customers saying?

Look at the journey Apple has made through the years and what they focused their unique experience on:

- Apple: changing the way the world communicates
  - "Byte into an Apple" (Late 1970s)
  - "Soon there will be 2 kinds of people. Those who use computers, and those who use Apples." (Early 1980s)
  - "The Computer for the rest of us" (1984)
  - "The Power to Be Your Best" (1990)
  - "Think different" (1997–2002)
  - "Switch" (2002–2003)
  - "Get a Mac" (2006-2009)

Apple seems to be cornering the market with their products *because* of the customer experience. They don't need to sell their products, because their marketing has already done this for them. You walk into an Apple store and you just want to be a part of what they are doing. They have focused on improving the customer experience by making the visual experience so amazing, their competitors cannot keep up. They have sailed away into unchartered territory because they have a unique experience you can only get from them (at least for now).

They have also mastered Emotional Branding—associating their brand so strongly with emotions so that it rises above just the product or service offered. It becomes an experience.

Marketer Marc Gobe, author of *Emotional Branding* and principal of d/g worldwide, said Apple's brand is the key to its survival. According to Gobe, emotional brands have three things in common:

✳ **The company projects a humanistic corporate culture and a strong corporate ethic, characterized by volunteerism, support of good causes or involvement in the community.** Nike blundered here when it was discovered that its shoes were made in Asian sweatshops. Apple, on the other hand, comes across as profoundly humanist. Its founding ethos was power to the people through technology, and it remains committed to computers in education. "It's always about people," Gobe said.

✳ **The company has a unique visual and verbal vocabulary, expressed in product design and advertising.** This is true of Apple. Its products and advertising are clearly recognizable. (So is Target's, or even Wal-Mart's, Gobe said.)

✳ **The company has established a "heartfelt connection" with its customers. This can take several forms, from building trust to establishing a community around a product.** In Apple's case, its products are designed around people: "Take the iPod, it brings an emotional, sensory experience to computing," Gobe said. "Apple's design is people-driven."

Gobe noted that Apple has always projected a human touch—from the charisma of Steve Jobs to the notion that its products are sold for a love of technology.[29]

---

5 Tips for Motivating 'WOW' in Your Clients

By **Misty Lown** (owner and CEO of Misty's Dance Unlimited, which is frequently recognized as one of the best in the dance studio industry and another of our model companies.)

1. SHOWCASE their achievements.

It doesn't even have to relate to your business. At my dance studio we recognize student dance achievements, but we don't stop there! We make announcements for students who are A+ Achievers in school, sports, and community. If we are about "more than just great dancing", it makes sense to showcase our clients who are, too!

2. TRAIN desired behaviors with rewards.

My son Mason is rewarded with prize tickets every time he shows progress at his orthodontist appointments. I could never motivate him to wear his retainer like those tickets do! And, it's not just kids who respond to rewards. If you have a frequent flier account or a credit card with miles, you have been trained as well!

(continued)

---

3. COMPLIMENT something about your client every time you see them—even if it's just their hair.

According to Dale Carnegie, the greatest desire of the human heart is to be important. Abraham Lincoln said it this way: "Everyone likes a compliment." So ask yourself when you are interacting with your clients—is your focus on what's great about YOU or what's great about THEM? If the 90/10 rule of giving vs. selling is important in social media, it's even more important in real time.

4. ASK clients for ideas about how to make your business more excellent.

When they tell you—and they will—act on as many suggestions as possible and then give credit where it is due. Harry S. Truman said, "It is amazing what you can accomplish if you do not care who gets the credit."

5. CREATE a tribe of ambassadors.

In his book *Tribe*, author Seth Godin says, "Ultimately, people are most easily lead where they want to go anyway." Everybody wants to be a part of a winning team. Not one of your clients wakes up in the morning and aspires to mediocrity. Find ways for your clients to get on board with, or be a part of, your winning team. Can they represent your brand with logo wear, accompany you to a function, serve on advisory board, committee, or referral project? Excellence breeds excellence. Make the most of your client-ambassadors.

The WOW Factor is unique to your company and brings your customers back to you time and time again because they loved the experience. They will also help to spread the word about it to their friends, family, and colleagues becoming your ambassadors or better yet, your Raving Fans. Identifying, or creating, your WOW Factor will create a market space that makes you completely unique.

■ The Transformation

It's not only about the experience... it's about the transformation you provide.

The transformation is all about the *unique* experience that you offer. It is clear that any product or service can be copied and it's just a matter of time before it is. However, and this is a *big* however, the interaction your customers have with you is unique because of the company culture and the people you have working with the company. Whether it's through the sales force, the customer service, or the online presence, there is only one company that can give the value that you do in the way that you do it! And, in some way, you are transforming their lives for the better.

It is a matter of knowing what that is and then clearly defining that for the market and your potential customers. How will they know what makes you special if you don't tell them or show them in some way.

As our world begins to change, we are seeing more and more of a "giving model" of doing business. Potential customers are able to get some sort of sample of what it is you offer so that they can determine if they want more. It may be a free ebook, a free report, a free session, a free sample... whatever it is, this gives value and, if done right, will make the customer want to come back for more.

TOMS Shoes is the global hero for the One For One model. They have integrated their giving into the core of how they are doing business. When you purchase a pair of shoes for yourself, you are giving a pair of shoes to a child in need. This transforms what historically would be a somewhat meaningless transaction into something far greater. Their customers are contributors to a greater cause and happily pay higher prices for the privilege of being a part of their movement.

It is the people in the company that *cannot* be duplicated—and that is what makes the company fully unique. Once we realize there are enough customers out in the world who need the service or solution that a company has to offer, and are able to communicate it in a way that ensures sales, the company has stepped away from the competitive model to a unique experience. There are elements that must be present in order to establish this.

- The company is clear on its purpose and why it is doing what it is doing.
- It is able to communicate this to the market.
- All the employees know the bigger purpose and are able to do their jobs with this in mind.
- The customers know that in order to have this experience, they must come to you.

■ What makes you different from everyone else?

Can you identify the key factors that differentiate you from everyone else out in the market? When you can clearly define those factors, you can start to play the game by rules you set. This is when you begin to create your own market and provide the best service to the customers that love what you do. Now wouldn't that be the best place to be?

Zappos decided early on to focus on customer service to differentiate them and make them stand out from all others. Because their focus is on providing the absolute best customer service, it has seeped into their entire culture, values, and way of doing business. They have been able to clearly define the experience they want their customers to receive. In one example, they tested their customer service department with someone calling in to order a pizza—which has nothing to do with shoes at all. But they were able to help and provide what their customer wanted. From the company's perspective, each chance they get to talk to their customers live, gives them a chance to strengthen their relationship with that person.

Once you have clearly defined exactly what makes you different, you can start to attract the people who need what you have. There is a change of mindset that needs to happen here to really grasp this.

Our world is built on a model of scarcity, but this is just a belief that has become ingrained into our cultures. One of the things we've started seeing in the business world is that when working with the model of "giving" and having a "greater purpose", the so-called limited market expands. The nature of the Universe is to always change and expand. So knowing that things are constantly changing and evolving will put you in front of the pack when you actively work with this. Collaborative markets are expanding because everyone is working together to increase the exposure.

This is a model that is seen quite clearly in Internet marketing. A company will often work with affiliates to promote their product or service... even their so-called competitors because they know that the more people who hear about a certain product or service, the more likely they will be to buy. Most likely not the first or second or even third time but when the time is right for that customer. Plus they also realize that a customer may not want a product now but the next time they'll be ready to purchase—and we have no control over that. So the company comes from an authentic place of service and information.

As the affiliates work together, they know that they are bringing value to their own markets and in turn expanding the market in general. Would you rather have a piece of the pie that is not growing but rather shrinking... or a piece of a dynamic and expanding pie? A smaller piece of a bigger pie is often better than a bigger piece of a disappearing pie. It's all about a change in mindset from a scarcity model to an abundant model, realizing that there really is enough for everyone out there! Especially when we give great value and collaborate with others to expand the pie.

TOMS has a competition where their customers (AKA Raving Fans) can apply to go on one of their giving trips where they actually give the shoes to the children in need. They choose fifty participants with the highest votes and give them a unique experience that they won't find anywhere else.

When you have something to offer that no one else has, and give a unique experience, where will the customers go? To you of course! By creating a very unique experience, you will keep people coming back for more *and* telling their friends about it too! This is the new experienced-based model in action... and it works like a charm!

Darren Hardy of Success Magazine says there is no competitive advantage in a satisfied customer: no word of mouth, no buzz, no loyalty. Customers have to be loved. To love is to **'WOW'**!

"I own a dance studio with over 700 students... I made it my goal to turn every interaction into a **'WOW'** experience! I went through my organization from top to bottom looking for ways to elevate our client experience."

'WOW' the client. "We evaluated every client (parent›s) touch point and every process they engaged in. We have made leagues of improvements to all of our processes, including online ticketing for recitals, automating all client accounts with software, online booking of private lessons, and adding a new enrollment management office. The leadership team was challenged to take every client interaction as an opportunity to make things right, better, or exceptional for students and their families."

'WOW' the end user (student). "To our elevated systems and customer service, we added 'WOW' opportunities for our students for the upcoming school year, including new performing groups, a guest choreographer from the hit TV show 'So You Think You Can Dance,' the opportunity to perform 'Nutcracker' live with our local Symphony (first time ever in our city!), hosting a regional dance competition featuring studios from three states, a free 15th Anniversary Celebration and Alumni Event, and a trip to NYC for our high school students so they can study with the best of the best!"

'WOW' the entire brand experience. "Even the physical building, which is only five years old, didn't escape the microscope. We repainted the entire building, remodeled the dressing rooms, filled the children's lobby with the best in children's literature, got new tables and chairs for our cafe, updated the stock and fixtures in our store, resealed the parking lot, and added a snack bar."

(continued)

'WOW' the community. "And, we didn't stop with our clients. We included the community by starting a non-profit foundation called 'A Chance to Dance Foundation,' which will provide scholarships for financial need, talent, and diversity so every child in our community will have 'a chance to dance'!

"The event has raised over $280,000 for the local chapter of the Red Cross in the first six years ($95,000 of it was raised last year). The results have been phenomenal! Last month we had over 4,700 people come to our Spring Recitals, and at our recent Fall Registration, we had people CAMPING OUT overnight to secure a premium spot in line. My daughter and I went out at 6:30 a.m. in white aprons to serve our families fresh pastries and coffee while they waited. The first person in line was surprised with balloons and a free registration, and everyone walked out with a free geranium that day. People ate it up...they love to be loved on!"

'WOW' Life. "Best of all, I just spent 10 days with my family in Florida, and am not due back in the office for two and half more weeks. Since attending the HPF, I have found that I can run my dance business remotely on about 4 hours per week of staff contact/communication for the times I want to travel or spend at home with kids. This kind of 'time wealth' is not only giving me precious memories with my family, but also the ability to pursue the new licensing business with vigor.

"Our motto at Misty's Dance Unlimited has always been 'More Than Just Great Dancing!' "

How can you add "WOW" to every one of your client touch points, throughout the entire client experience, with your brand and business? The answer to that question is what will allow you to have a "WOW" life, too.

Misty Lown is the owner and CEO of Misty's Dance Unlimited, which is frequently recognized as one of the best in the dance studio industry. For more information, visit **www.mistysdance.com**

2. Full Engagement

To engage is to occupy one's full attention: to attract and hold fast. An "engaged employee" is one who is wholeheartedly involved and enthusiastic about their work, and thus will act in a way that furthers their organization's interests. When an employee has passion and purpose for what they do, using their talents, they are able to reach their full potential.

Employee engagement is truly one of the most important keys to maximizing performance in any organization today. *To get a clear picture of the current work environment, we need to share some statistics we discovered in our research on employee engagement.*

■ Employees who are engaged are more productive, creative, and loyal

There are numerous studies that show how when an employee is engaged—that is, they really enjoy what they do—they will be more productive, feel better about their job, and be a part of the vision for the company. They will stay longer with the company and contribute on a daily basis to making the company excel.

Here are some alarming figures that we surfaced:

- In one global survey, just 21 percent of staff reported that they are fully engaged at their workplace. Professor Gary Hamel of London Business School commented on this, "the other 79 percent may be physically on the job, but they've left their enthusiasm and ingenuity at home."[30]
- Only 22 percent of U.S. employees are engaged *and* thriving.[31]

- This is a huge waste and also a huge opportunity. If that level of engagement can be increased, then productivity and innovation can rocket. Not only is this possible but it can also be done at a far lower cost than many of the investments that companies engage in to improve their businesses.

- The 2013 Gallup report on employee engagement estimates that active disengagement costs between $450 billion to $550 billion per year—and that is just in the United States only.

- Companies that experience high engagement also experience 147 percent higher earnings per share.[32]

- In a global report from HR consultancy Tower Perrins in 2006, based on surveys of over 600,000 staff members in a wide range of industries, "Companies with high levels of employee engagement improved 19.2 percent in operating income while companies with low levels of employee engagement declined 32.7 percent over the study period."[33]

- 70 percent of engaged employees indicate they have a good understanding of how to meet customer needs; only 17 percent of non-engaged employees say the same.[34]

- 78 percent of engaged employees would recommend their company's products or services, against 13 percent of the disengaged.[35]

- When companies successfully engage both their customers and employees, they experience a 240 percent boost in performance-related business outcomes compared with an organization with neither engaged employees nor engaged customers.[36]

Clearly employee engagement makes a big difference on the output and the revenues of a company.[37] By not having fully engaged employees, a company is simply walking away from significant profits.[38] It's like leaving money on the table that could otherwise be used to help grow the company.[39]

Not only that, it is hurting countries that are trying to recover from the economic crisis and return to the prosperity levels experienced before the recession. Lack of engagement isn't only a problem in the corporate world, it is a serious problem that should also be addressed from a national level as well. "Gallup's analysis suggests that the most successful organizations effectively engage their employees, leading to higher productivity and better financial outcomes. These organizations appear to move the job market in the right direction."[40] There seems to be a significant link between engagement and job creation.

Here are some simple questions to ask yourself to gage your personal level of engagement (and be honest about it!):

1. In percentage terms, how much of what you do at work is 'play'?
2. In percentage terms, how much of what you do at work is 'work'?
3. In percentage terms, how much of what you do at work is 'misery'?

Gallup has performed the Q12 surveys for thousands of clients and can benchmark norms by industry and identify whether or not a firm has engaged, unengaged or disengaged employees. They have found that 71 percent of employees are either disengaged or actively disengaged. Apparently middle-aged college-educated workers are the most disengaged of all.[41] (see Apendix A for more details)

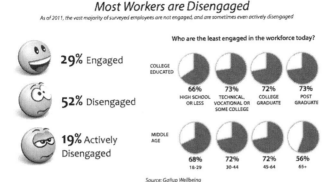

The Sad Truth

Most Workers are Disengaged

As of 2011, the vast majority of surveyed employees are not engaged, and are sometimes even actively disengaged

29% Engaged

52% Disengaged

19% Actively Disengaged

Who are the least engaged in the workforce today?

COLLEGE EDUCATED

| 66% | 73% | 72% | 73% |
| HIGH SCHOOL OR LESS | TECHNICAL, VOCATIONAL OR SOME COLLEGE | COLLEGE GRADUATE | POST GRADUATE |

MIDDLE AGE

| 68% | 72% | 72% | 56% |
| 18-29 | 30-44 | 45-64 | 65+ |

Source: Gallup Wellbeing

An interesting question then arises: is engagement contagious? There is, indeed, some experimental evidence for such a process of emotional contagion. Barsade (2002) conducted an innovative laboratory study in which the transfer of moods among people in a group and its influence on performance was examined.[42]

There are many studies that show how emotions are easily contagious and you can experiment with this yourself. Be observant of others moods and see how they affect you. When you have a high percentage of the organization feeling nervous, fearful, uncertain, it definitely affects the workplace. And likewise, the opposite is true, too: when you have a high percentage who are enthused, excited, and motivated, this also will spread. This is why so many companies are actively working on culture transformation and one of the most effective ways to accomplish a positive, Thriving Culture is through working actively with employee engagement.

- ***Employee engagement can boost loyalty.*** A study by the Corporate Executive Board found engaged employees committed to their companies gave 57 percent more effort, and were 87 percent less likely to resign, than workers who said they were disengaged.[43]

Employees, who are enthusiastic and contributing to moving the company forward, feel a stronger sense of purpose and are more likely to stay longer with an organization. They feel better and are able to contribute on a higher capacity.

---

3 Levels of Commitment

There are different levels of commitment of the individual. Here we have described them to the extreme examples. However, most people will fall into some moderation of these three areas. Who do you want to be working with in your organization?

1. **Just the Paycheck**—these employees are the ones who live for the weekends and dread Mondays. They are there to put in their time, get their paycheck, so that they can go do what they would rather be doing. These individuals lack motivation, enthusiasm, purpose, and drive, and often do the least amount work for the least amount of effort. You will also find those who do work hard but are barely making ends meet, and sometimes these individuals will even have more than one job. They end up exhausted and stressed. Either type is not very happy with their lives.

2. **Career Driven**—these employees are very focused, determined, hard working, and ambitious. They do a good and even great job and often climb the ladder quickly to get into management and executive level positions. But they also tend to be working on their own agenda and striving to get to the top at all costs. Often they are either

(continued)

---

stepping on others to get there or sacrificing other areas of their lives such as family life or marriages because of their hard driving efforts. They are often stressed, not necessarily taking care of themselves physically, and certainly not living a balanced life. They would be considered "Type A" and can burn out and have stress-related health issues, such as heart attacks, strokes, etc. These are the people who often face a mid-life crisis that shakes their world and has them re-evaluating their path, purpose, and meaning in life.

3. **It's a Calling!**—these individuals are so passionate about what they are doing, they would do it without getting paid. They have come to realize that the work they are doing is what they were meant to do. They, too, tend to work hard and are ambitious... but to them work is play, so it doesn't affect their health in such a detrimental way. They have lots of energy and are constantly excited about their progress. They have a big vision and know that what they are doing is positively impacting the world in some way. They feel very connected to their purpose—they know why they are doing what they are doing and it feels wonderful. Even if they might work long hours, they do tend to lead a more balanced life. It can be just because they are so joyful in their work, it spills over into the other areas of their lives as well.

■ Increased productivity

Engaged employees simply are more productive. Since they are enjoying what they are doing, the creativity and feeling of contribution will increase. The Japanese have a philosophy which understands that, just as in nature, a company is like a living organism. It is constantly changing and growing and therefore the employees are always looking for new ways to improve whatever their scope of work may be. In production, a saving of a few seconds in a production line by improving efficiency can increase the output tenfold.

Wikipedia explains: "**Kaizen** (改善?), Japanese for "improvement", or "change for the better" refers to a philosophy or practices that focus upon continuous improvement of processes in manufacturing, engineering, game development, and business management."

Kaizen is a daily process, the purpose of which goes beyond simple productivity improvement. It is also a process that, when done correctly, humanizes the workplace, eliminates overly hard work ("muri"), and teaches people how to perform experiments on their work using the scientific method and how to learn to spot and eliminate waste in business processes.

Employee wellbeing is also important in the results of an employee's work.

- Employees report they are too stressed to be effective. According to a ComPsych Survey, two-thirds of workers report high stress levels, affecting their ability to be productive.[44]
- Employee health and wellbeing are critical for the financial wellbeing of an organization. A study done by the World Economic Forum, in conjunction with Right

Management, contends that when health and wellbeing are promoted at work, employees are eight times more likely to be engaged and organizations are three times more likely to be productive.

Change management and wellbeing expert Fran Melmed of Context Communication Consulting says, "There is renewed reason to pay attention to employee engagement and wellbeing." [45]

■ Recruit for attitude and value match; train for skill

Make sure the personality fits with the culture and values of the organization. This will increase the likelihood of a long term employment, job satisfaction, and higher productivity. Skills can be learned; personality and attitude cannot.

This is also not to say that you only hire the same type of people. Diversity is important to ensure creativity and innovation. But having the same values and beliefs in the common goals are essential for the organization. In a hiring process, we have seen companies that will pass by a candidate who has the experience to instead hire someone who has the drive and motivation and can be taught. There is an inherent risk—and the start up may take more time—but, in the longer run, if the person was a right hire based on personality and passion, they will be more productive over time. It's a strategic move on their part for the longer investment and belief in a person's ability to contribute to the company.

One of the very common traits with Amazing Companies is that they are very focused on recruiting people with the right value match for the organization. In talking with several employees of one of our model companies, Achievers, they were very aware of the company culture and how important it is to bring people on board who have the same values. We heard consistently that it's the people that are making the difference in company. Having the right environment, a Thriving Culture, and value match of the employees and the company brings enthusiasm into a business, making full engagement much easier to accomplish.

With the alarming statistics showing that upwards of eighty percent of employees do not necessarily like their jobs, it is critical to find ways to engage and inspire all employees to maximize their happiness and wellbeing, which will directly impact their productivity to much higher levels. They go hand in hand and must be addressed for the wellbeing of the entire organization.

3. Flow

When you've worked on the foundational elements of a company, such as discovering the purpose and passions of your people, you can start to regularly achieve a state of flow. This can be reached on an individual basis and on an organizational level as well.

Mihaly Csikszentmihalyi, a noted psychology professor and author of several books, is most well known for his notion of flow, with years of research and writing about this topic. Flow is simply defined as a type of happiness in which someone loses the sense of time, self-consciousness, and even self.

Many different areas have their own name referring to this state of flow. In music, they say "in the groove". With sports, it is called being "in the zone". In Buddhism, you will hear "being one with things", and when you are around professional poker players, they say "playing the A-game". We have expressions such as *go with the flow, on the ball, in the moment, being present, on a roll, wired in, on fire, in tune,* or *centered*; all of which are referring to a similar state of being.

Wikipedia defines flow as "the mental state of operation in which a person in an activity is fully immersed in a feeling of energized focus, full involvement, and success in the process of the activity."

Flow is a state of supreme creativity

Clearly it is an ultimate state to reach. The question is, how to get there? The formula is quite simple, with two steps:

1. Be happy in the "now".
2. Have a vision of the future.

Vishen Lakhiani gave a great talk about happiness being the new productivity. In it, he describes that when looking at flow on an individual level, there are four states of mind to consider.[46]

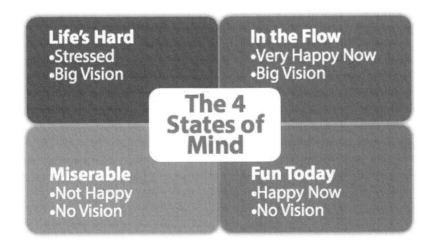

In order to achieve flow, Csikszentmihalyi lays out the following eight conditions:

1. Goals are clear
2. Feedback is immediate
3. A balance between opportunity and capacity
4. Concentration deepens
5. The present is what matters
6. Control is no problem
7. The sense of time is altered
8. The loss of ego

When these conditions are met, you can reach the state of flow. The purpose to describing flow in such depth is because you reach optimal productivity in this state. This is important for companies to realize and to work toward allowing employees the environment and opportunity to be as productive as possible.

When you begin to have key elements in place—like the right environment, the right state of mind, the excitement and focus—you can reach a state of flow individually... and this can also happen within an organization. This is organizational flow, and it acts as an accelerator within the business. Similar to building a house, it is important to have a solid foundation within an organization. This always takes the most time, but, when done properly, it allows for the rest of the building to happen quickly and smoothly.

The foundation to having an Amazing Company includes being clear on the vision, having shared values that you can live and work by, giving your team the opportunity to shine and grow, and creating a Thriving Culture which, in turn, gives your customers a unique experience they want to come back for again and again.

As you work on certain key foundational elements, you will begin to see that other elements will fall into place easily and naturally.

Eventually it will lead to a state of flow and you will find yourself and your business in the upward spiral of expansion, joy, passion, excitement, higher productivity, and higher profits, as well as making a bigger impact. When you have reached organizational flow, things happen in an accelerated manner. Let's discuss the building blocks it takes to reach organizational flow specifically.

1. Systems

A company is a system of systems working together to create the whole. We are not here to get into all the different operational systems in a company, as our focus is on the people within the organization. Just as our bodies have many systems running at the same time to keep us functioning, an organization has different departments and teams making the company expand and grow. The systems are both the foundation and the structure of the company to allow for growth and development. Without solid systems, the foundation is not strong, and when growth does happen, it can be quite unstable, or, worse, even collapse, because it was not set up with optimal systems.

The focus of the Evoloshen Program is not to help you put the systems in place, because our clients already have many of them in place. But as we work through the exercises of our program, there will be improvements in many of the systems to reach a higher level of performance both for the employees and also for the organization. However, we do want to call attention to the fact that the business must be systematized in order to be sustainable and to handle significant growth. There are many wonderful resources, such as *The E-Myth* by Michael Gerber, to explore how to build your systems within your business.

2. Engagement

We've discussed the importance of having full engagement within an organization and allowing people to focus on their strengths and passions. If everyone in a company is doing this, the results multiply tenfold at least! Allow for open expression, development, and creativity to abound. There are dozens of studies showing the results on the bottom line of how important it is to have engaged employees. The more enthusiasm and focus, the better the performance will be. When individuals know what to do and really put their hearts into it, they are able to progress rapidly.

It is essential for an organization to find ways to get the employees excited about what they are doing. Having a shared-value system is the foundation to get started. Then it is important that each employee understands the importance of their role in the organization. It is possible to inspire even the most mundane tasks to greatness when they see how it fits into the bigger picture. Valuing, or giving recognition, is one of the easiest ways to help people feel worthy. It is important to also work toward matching their job duties to those that fit their strengths and talents. That will make it easy for them to then succeed.

By investing some time and effort to the individuals to make them feel that what they do is actually making a difference, they will blossom and grow and, often, exceed their expectations to delivering amazing results.

When participating in the Evoloshen Program, one Amazing Employee is selected who has performed and contributed in huge ways to the shift in the organization. This gives the employees an incentive to be a part of an amazing transformation. And what often happens within the company shifts the personal lives in positive ways for the participants as well, giving hidden benefits to the wellbeing of the people in the process.

3. Collaboration

Collaboration is the new currency. Businesses that understand the importance of collaboration and that work together with other businesses are able to grow rapidly and reach more people with their offerings. The same magic happens internally when the company employees work together to support each other with the same common mission.

As we have mentioned, collaboration is more than teamwork—it is having the shared vision and comes from a place of service. It means having an understanding of the Bigger Purpose and keeping that at the forefront of all decisions, actions, and results. When people work together for a common goal, the sum is greater than the individual parts. It is possible to achieve greater results, faster, and more effectively when a collaborative effort is involved.

Collaboration within a company is essential to reach organizational flow.

4. Thriving Culture

We cannot stress on the importance of creating a Thriving Culture in a company. This is one of the biggest elements to creating A Most Amazing Company. It is what will attract the right top-talent to the company and what will keep them longer term. It will allow for the growth and development of the individuals and the groups and teams, and will push the organization to evolve in the greatest version of itself.

A Thriving Culture will keep innovation and creativity flowing and will lead to amazing results and a huge contribution to the world.

5. FLOW

All these factors—systems, engagement, collaboration and a Thriving Culture—will lead to flow.

Flow in business happens when the employees are happy and when they feel cared for and valued by their supervisors and company. It is when the employees are reaching their maximum potential and the company's productivity accelerates. It is the upwards spiral of doing business because the deals are done, the innovations come forth, a positively charged environment exists with high enthusiasm and a sense of accomplishment—all of which motivates the entire organization. One of Csikszentmihalyi's preconditions for flow is to set goals that employees can actually achieve. And very importantly, no interruptions! People are best in flow when they can focus.

When a person reaches the flow state, they feel great and productive. When a company achieves flow, it reaches amazing results. The company is on track to being an Amazing Company! And then flow is the accelerator that makes it all happen faster, more effectively, and better than anyone expected. It is finding that zone of amazingness. It is a state that any company would love to be in, and it *is* achievable!

10

People

> "Our people are our single greatest strength and most enduring long term competitive advantage." —*Gary Kelly, CEO Southwest Airlines*

Without people working together, we wouldn't have companies that are growing and bringing value to the world. It's as simple as that. As we've said, we believe that people are the greatest asset of any organization. Without the people, the company would not be able to exist.

These days, it's easier for individuals to start up their own companies. The ability to reach a global market is easier than ever. In fact, the largest group becoming entrepreneurs are women, where the latest studies show that for every ten men starting a business, there are 8 women—a trend that is likely to continue.[47]

It was interesting to see Instagram sold to Facebook for $1 Billion after only eighteen months in business with thirteen employees, zero revenues, and over 100 million registered users in 2012. If we look at just the numbers, that makes the value on average of each of the 13 employees almost worth approximately $77 million—the highest valuation of employee value to date as we write this book. Not bad for Mike Krieger and Kevin Systrom, the young entrepreneurs who started Instagram. Back in the late 1990s we had the IT bubble where company valuations were very high and, unfortunately, often they were not able to deliver the value due to the level of market maturity. The value of Instagram, however, is in the reach and in the number of users. Again, the world is changing due to technology, and it probably won't be long before we see a company sell where the average employee value is over $100 million.

The reason for this example is not to put a price tag on employees at all, but more to show the power of the people, both with the entrepreneurs and with their global reach. The market has changed forever and now the ability to enter new markets and be competitive has never been easier. Reaching customers in this day and age is easy; the global market is at our fingertips with our laptops and smart phones. Connecting to and bringing valuable content to people is where the value is today.

That connection to people is what is making Amazing Companies thrive, both with the employees and with their customers. As much as technology is supposed to be making our lives easier, faster, and more efficient, the bottom line is that we are humans sharing an experience on this planet and we need to connect to each other on a deeper level. It makes our lives meaningful. People are not to be considered *property* or something that can be used. They need to be valued and appreciated. They need to be given the opportunity to thrive and be the best that they can be. When companies offer this to their employees, they transform a company into a place of growth and development where they, in turn, can connect to the customers and give a unique experience and WOW them so that they become Raving Fans as well.

Let's explore the importance of Recognition and Appreciation, how to create a Magnetic Tribe attracting the right people, and a Thriving Culture, where employees are reaching their full potential and productivity.

1. Recognition & Appreciation

As human beings, we like to be appreciated and recognized, whether it's at home, at school, or at work. A *big* reason individuals seek to leave a company is because they do not feel valued. It is always surprising how little a person's work is acknowledged in an organization. Just on a personal level, who likes to feel like they've been taken advantage of or taken for granted? No one! Why should this be any different in the work place?

In an online survey by Harris Interactive:

> *"Almost all employees (93 percent) who reported feeling valued said that they are motivated to do their best at work and 88 percent reported feeling engaged. This compares to just 33 percent and 38 percent, respectively, of those who said they do not feel valued. Among employees who feel valued, just one in five (21 percent) said they intend to look for a new job in the next year (vs. 50 percent of those who said that they do not feel valued)."[48]*

Valuing employees is essential to retention—workers who feel valued, according to the Psychologically Healthy Workplace Program, "are more likely to report better physical and mental health, as well as higher levels of engagement, satisfaction and motivation, compared to those who do not feel valued by their employers". As a company grows, it's essential to put systems into place that give recognition and valuing of the employees.

Recognizing and appreciating employees is a simple retention strategy that gives back tenfold and had a direct positive impact on the bottom line. Employees are more motivated by receiving recognition than monetary rewards or pay increases. A salary increase has increased benefits on average of three months whereas a public recognition, such as employee of the month, has increased benefits upwards of eighteen months!

Let's explore how you can best appreciate your employees, coworkers, and management.

■ Celebrate accomplishments

As a generalization, we do not celebrate enough! In a corporate environment, yes, we do celebrate reaching our targets and goals, but what about the path to reach it. This is filled with lots of smaller accomplishments that made it possible to reach the larger target. Why aren't we celebrating each and every small win? Doing so in a company creates a culture of fun, recognition, adoration, and joy. It spreads happiness and makes others want to contribute and be a part of, or even better, the cause of the celebration.

Don't just wait for the end of the year holiday party, or landing a new big client; find ways to foster a celebratory culture that will make everyone happy to be a part of. Find ways of acknowledging individuals, teams, accomplishments, improvements, anything and everything you can think of because this will spread within the company. It will raise moral and instill a desire to contribute more and receive some of the recognition.

It is human nature to want to feel loved and appreciated. A simple "thank you" goes a long way! This should become a regular part of doing business. And not just for employees either—celebrate your customers, your partners, the UPS man who delivers the packages on time, the janitor who is always in the background making sure the office is clean for everyone. A little adoration goes a long, long way to increasing productivity and bringing a sense of fun into the environment!

> "You don't stop laughing because you grow old, you grow old because you stop laughing." — *Michael Pritchard*

Celebrating also brings a focus to what is going right. This will ensure that even more goes right, and it becomes fun for everyone. Somewhere along our evolution we decided to focus on the negative aspects of life. Our minds are conditioned to look at the problems, the demands, the challenges, and the fears, instead of focusing on the solutions, the ease, the answers, and the joy. When we learn to change our focus to the more positive, those things will also change and become more positive as well.

■ Have ability to develop & grow

Most companies do take into consideration some sort of career path or growth within a company. The question here is how much of this is related to an individual's passions and personal purpose? It's great to invest in improving skills and allowing people to grow professionally. It is important to ask how this is in alignment with a person's passions. If learning certain skills will improve a job they are already bored at, is that the best investment? Investing in personal development—not professional skills, but life skills—will improve the wellbeing of a person in general.

Mentoring is a wonderful way to pass on knowledge and give a younger person a hand up. In an article by Darren Hardy, the visionary force behind SUCCESS magazine as its publisher and editorial director, he shares an interesting concept: reverse mentoring. This is where a younger person can teach an older person things about technology and how the younger people are thinking these days. Some interesting facts about the changing work environment:

- We will soon have five generations in the workplace—all at once.
- Millennials (born between 1977 and 1997) will account for half of all the employees in the world by 2014.

With reverse mentoring, you can also have women teach men some of the communication and social and interpersonal skills that women are more naturally adept at, and how a man should best communicate to, work with, and help support women in the workplace. This reverse mentoring will teach both ways and develop better relationships and understanding of the differences. Mentoring is one of the most efficient ways to pass knowledge and guidance, plus gain support and understanding, within an organization. One of the best ways for you to feel better yourself is to help others, and mentoring certainly gives a person that opportunity.

Zappos has a concept they call the Zappos Pipeline. Rather than focusing on individuals as assets (who can then leave), they focus on building a pipeline of people in every department with varying levels of skills and experience, ranging from entry level all the way up to management and leadership positions. Zappos makes most hires at the entry level and provide all the necessary training and mentorship necessary to become a senior leader within five to seven years.

The Big Goal at Zappos is that the employees think of their work not as a job or career, but as a calling. Zappos is growing and grooming their people, giving them challenges, investing in their personal growth through ongoing education and personal development programs, all within a Thriving Culture that gives them a high level of retention and makes them an Amazing Company! It is a new mindset that is emerging and it is paying off handsomely for these Amazing Companies that are working consciously with it.

■ Develop fun systems for recognition

Work together from within the organization to come up with fun ways to celebrate and recognize accomplishments. You can have contests, declare a day of appreciation for women/men, ring bells when sales are made, give out prizes... really the sky is the limit here! This is a place to engage the entire company in creating a culture that they buy into and consider fun. Allow the employees to be creative and make suggestions and then choose which ones make sense. Having some sort of visual ways to show progress are also great. It reinforces why you are doing what you are doing, where you are going, how far you've come, and how far you have left to go.

When I (Karin) started in executive search, we had a "chip board" where we hung different colored chips at the end of each work day that were carried over to track the whole week. It became a fun game to see how many chips we could hang at the end of the day and of course, everyone wanted to beat out the top performers. This naturally made everyone more productive—just because we had a visual way of checking on everyone's progress each day and week.

You can have a company or department vision board where each employee writes down what they want to have in their lives, what experiences, and how they want to contribute. When everyone knows each other's dreams and goals, the group will begin to support each other to achieve their own success.

Another trend we discovered is how many of these Amazing Companies are changing the titles of positions. This helps to eliminate the traditional hierarchal thinking or broaden the scope of the job. For example, instead of being called CEO, Blake Mckoskie is dubbed "Chief Shoe Giver"; Doug Piwinski is the "Sole Singer", which is TOMS speak for senior vice president, marketing and communication. We found that what would be equivalent to a

VP of human resources in Virgin is called "Head of Group People Strategy" or "People Directors"; at Southwest Airlines: "Chief People Officer"; and at Choice Hotels: "Director of Passion". Even housekeeping has been elevated at Choice Hotels to be called "the style department" because they are styling the rooms. Now that must make those employees feel proud to be a part of that team. We, the authors, have been inspired by this trend, so Karin is officially the "Chief Joy Bringer" and Sergio is "Chief Inspiration Partner". And we found many companies having employees responsible specifically for the culture with various titles such as "Chief Culture Officers". The titles are often fun and are certainly a conversation starter to figure out exactly what that means.

We want to stress that fun is a very subjective idea. What is fun for one may not be for another. Each company is made of up a group of very varied individuals. This is why the answers *must* come from within the group. If the manager, CEO, or MD just decides that a dinner at a local restaurant is the way to incorporate fun into the company, the group does not have a vested interest—it's wasn't their idea. But when the group is the one that comes up with the suggestions and ideas, then success, interaction, commitment, and involvement will definitely be higher. People will own what they create.

Achievers has created a software system that helps organizations develop the behavioral changes to make recognition easy and fun. By using their system branded to each company, employees can see very easily who is accomplishing—and getting recognized— exactly what in the company. What is so powerful about their system is that it isn't only the management that is responsible for the pats on the back, the employees get the chance to give recognition as well. And this makes for a very engaged, supportive environment that is focusing on what is going well.

Give the people the power to decide and watch what can happen! This is one of the best places to spark creativity. And having creative people will definitely bring about more innovative ideas and often the discussions that take place at these fun "non-work" hours end up being about work. Many of our designated Most Amazing Company models have implemented significant profit producing ideas that originated from off-hours discussions.

2. Magnetic Tribe

■ Create a mystique that everyone wants to be a part of

A tribe is a group of people that band together for the common good of the group. According to Seth Godin's definition, "A tribe is a group of people connected to one another, connected to a leader, and connected to an idea. For millions of years, human beings have been part of one tribe or another. A group needs only two things to be a tribe: a shared interest and a way to communicate."

A Magnetic Tribe is one that others want to be a part of. There is an attraction that is making people want to become a member. There are three critical factors to this:

- The people who are in the tribe love it and are raving about it—their happiness to be a part of this shows and acts as a magnet.
- The culture of the tribe is drawing people towards it because they want to find out more. There is a mystique that acts as a magnet and pulls people towards it to get more information, often times without the person even knowing why. They just want a part of it.
- The purpose of why they are doing what they are doing is bigger than they are; there is a bigger reason for existing and this attracts the right people like bees to honey.

A big problem that Malaysia has is its diminishing workforce, as people leave the country to get educated or find jobs in other parts of the world, rarely returning home afterwards. Normally, a company based in Kuala Lumpur would have difficulty recruiting from a global market for a number of reasons. MindValley has been able to create such a strong magnetic tribe and culture and has informed a global market about how great it is to work there, that they have hundreds of applicants for their openings. They have also changed a typical recruitment process to include a YouTube video application. The company has over a hundred employees from more than thirty countries. Because of some of these strategies, it has become a very sought after company to work for and attracts top talent globally.

---

10 Tips for Motivating 'WOW' in Your Employees

By Misty Lown (owner and CEO of Misty's Dance Unlimited)

1. SET the pace and standard for your organization.

If you are early, your employees will be early.
If you are efficient, they will be efficient.
If you pursue excellence with vigor, they will run hard to keep up with you!

At the end of the night at the dance studio, my administrative director asked a work-study student if she had taken out the garbage. She replied, "Well, I got it in the dumpster, but not really to the 'Misty standard'." Now, we do not have an official policy about how to put the garbage in the dumpster, but this 16 year old student knew enough about me to know that getting in half way, and not being able to shut the top, would not meet my standard!

As a leader, YOU are the measure of excellence for every facet of your organization whether it's cleanliness or communications.

(continued)

---

2. Be crystal CLEAR.

There is a verse in the Bible (Proverbs 29:18) that says, "Where there is no vision, the people perish." Now lack of vision may not cause someone to die at their desk, but it can certainly lead to death of an organization. As a leader, your job is to communicate your vision for the organization to every level of your team. They can't execute what they don't understand.

3. GET IN the trenches.

I love to jump into a class at a dance studio and show the teachers and students how I like it done. No amount of staff training will ever beat seeing a live demonstration of company standards in action. Getting your hands dirty will give you a greater appreciation of the work your staff does as well.

4. ACKNOWLEDGE contributions.

If there is a quality you value, find a way to recognize it in your people.

In his book "1,001 Ways to Reward Employee's", author Bob Nelson says the guidelines are simple: 1. Match the reward to the person, 2. Match the reward to the achievement, and 3. Be timely and specific. To that list I would add, "Be sincere." A handwritten note will never go out of style.

(continued)

5. If recognition is good, INCENTIVES are great.

If you've been through the recent issue of *SUCCESS*, you know that we are a culture of gamers. It doesn't matter whether it's Mario Kart or a company sponsored trip, we are wired to desire the next level. Even Dave Ramsey, who is known more for saving than spending, says that if he could find a way to do it, he would incentivize every position in his company.

6. COMMUNICATE consistently.

With a five kids to care for, I am not on site every day at my business. So, when I do have face time with employees I ask them some version of these same three questions every time:

1. Where are you winning?
2. What do you need my support on, or an answer on?
3. What idea do you have to make this place the best place to work and teach kids in the world?

This is a technique I picked up from reading about mega church pastor and author of "The Purpose Driven Life", Rick Warren. It works for a congregation of tens of thousands, and it works for my team of 22.

7. Give direction and GET OUT of the way.

Navy Captain D. Michael Abrashoff, author of "It's Your Ship: Management Techniques from the Best Damn Ship in the Navy" says, "The best way to keep a ship-or any organization-on course for success is to give the troops all the responsibility they can handle and then stand back."

(continued)

8. Keep it SIMPLE.

Dave Ramsey has three to five Key Results Areas (KRA's) for each position on his team. KRA's are how an employee knows if they are winning on your team. Mine are initiative, courtesy, follow through, excellence, problem solving. Good KRA's are few and firm.

9. Recognize that money is *not* the MOST MOTIVATING factor.

Years ago I conducted an anonymous (and free!) survey of my employees through the Department of Labor. Through this study, we found the following things to be most important (in order): Meaningful work, recognition, growth opportunity, and financial opportunity. Gone are the days when college grads are going to come out school and work a job they hate for 40 years, 40 hours a week just because it pays the bills.

Which leads to the most IMPORTANT thing:

10. Create opportunities for MEANINGFUL WORK.

In our organization we support what matters to employees with time off to volunteer, the freedom to create new programs, donated rehearsal space, and program sponsorships. Our teachers have created programs to connect generations through nursing home performances, a free dance outreach called Steps of Praise, school outreach programs and career days, and choreography for the local community theater. We even had one teacher volunteer to teach social dancing to the special education program at a local high school so that they could go confidently to the prom. Talk about "More than just great dancing!"

There are a lot of tools here, but here's the take away:
If you want excellence in your people, be relentless in your pursuit of it yourself.

You can't take people where you have never been.

■ Like attracts like

In the personal development world, there is a Universal Law that is often referred to as the Law of Attraction, which is simply defined as "like attracts like". That definition is a bit over simplified and the whole Law of Attraction idea has gotten a lot of criticism because it hasn't been completely understood or implemented.

But no one can deny that like-minded people enjoy being together and "birds of a feather flock together". A company culture will attract the type of people who will enjoy being there. In our years of experience as headhunters, we always matched a candidate's personality to the company culture first. That was the most critical match because if you don't have a strong match there, the person will never stay long-term, no matter how good the pay or position is.

Now, not every single person is going to be the same personality because you'll then create a culture of sameness. Diversity in a culture is what makes it interesting. There must be key elements that everyone has in common in order to create that bond and that common mission. When the purpose of the company is bigger and clearly defined—and the employees, customers, and partners buy into it—that's when you start to get a very dynamic and productive environment.

Look for people that complement each other and bring a healthy diversity into a company.

■ Positive association—you've got something they want

Again, what makes a company magnetic is the unique experience and the bigger reason for what you do. When you have a positive association, such as a clear message in how you are giving back to the world, you attract people to the company. Everyone knows that an unhappy customer won't come back for more because they have had some sort of negative association with the product or service and the opposite is true. If you give a positive experience to a customer, they will be back for more and even help you grow by recommending their friends or colleagues to you.

It's essential to have a positive image, a positive message, and a positive experience for anyone who has any contact with your organization. Because with the power of social media, if a customer has a negative experience, it can become a brand and PR nightmare, which no company would ever want to experience.

- David Carroll, a country western musician wrote a song called "United Breaks Guitars" about a very negative experience he had with an airline and posted a video on YouTube.
  - He wanted to reach one million views in a year; got there in four days because it went viral!
  - Over 150 million people know this story because of his creative use of social media.
  - Within four days, the stocks of United dropped 10 percent, or approximately $180 million (that amount would have purchased 51,000 guitars).[49]
  - With over eleven million views and counting, it has changed the landscape of customer service forever!
  - His video was even named one of the five most important videos in Google's history.
  - He has written a book about this called *United Breaks Guitars: The Power of One Voice in the Age of Social Media* and now speaks publically about this.
  - This has revolutionized the customer service industry.

More recently, Abercrombie and Fitch became a hot topic as the CEO made comments about being absolutely exclusionary because their ideal target customers are the cool, popular kids in school, and therefore, they don't carry larger sizes. Facing social media backlash, a video produced by Greg Karber said the company needed a brand readjustment, and he started a movement to give their expensive brand clothing to the homeless. The video went viral with over seven million views in 10 days.[50]

Unfortunately, it was easier to find negative messages that had gone viral versus positive ones. This means a company must be vigilant in making sure that the marketing message, what the employees are saying about the company, and what the customers experience are all in positive alignment with each other.

We did find one recent example of a brilliant use of social media. Caroline Williams, the CEO of Bodyform (a UK trademark of SCA: a global hygiene and paper company) responded in a very tongue and cheek manner with a YouTube video to a Facebook post about how the company had lied to men regarding that time of the month all women face. The original Facebook comment was very comical but their video response was even funnier, as Caroline admits they purposely misled the public in their advertising because they wanted to protect men from knowing the truth since they couldn't handle it. It went viral with over three million views. This is an excellent example of how social media can be used in a positive way to carry on the conversation; hence, build a relationship with millions.[51]

Zappos and MindValley both work actively with keeping their company open and their messages, experiences, and employee feedback consistent with their purpose. Because both companies understand the trend towards transparency, they just go ahead and make everything available and open for anyone to read.

- Ask Anything monthly newsletter at Zappos—any questions are asked anonymously and answered
- Zappos Culture book is published each year so it's not only for the entire company; it is for the entire world!
- MindValley started MindValley Insights where they decided to "open source" everything they do to the world. They share videos of what has worked for them and why. By sharing, they raise the bar but also tell the world what they are doing, which ends up attracting even more people to their company.

Transparency is a trend that will continue to grow and spread, perhaps much to the chagrin of those still stuck in the old industrial mindset that information is power and can be controlled. It has been sad to see some great brands damaged by the greed or unscrupulous behaviors of a few top leaders. It can take years to recover!

The power is shifting towards the people and this is a big part of what is driving the change to full transparency. After numerous scandals such as Enron, WorldCom, and the banking industry bailouts, integrity and authenticity are fully apparent—and expected—with the rise of sharing information.

- HCL in the spirit of creating trust through transparency created on online forum where they decided to have all financial information easily available for everyone, instead of the compartmentalized need-to-know basis that has been standard in traditional companies.
- Achievers is also completely open about its finances and has a daily meeting at 11:51 a.m. where the CFO shares all numbers with the entire company.

It is not only with the financial and cultural information. We are seeing trends that will be affecting the supplier chain in various consumer markets.

- Whole Foods is leading the battle towards transparency with GMO's (genetically modified organisms) in stating that by 2018, it will be required that all genetically modified foods are properly labeled as such.

- Many retail chains such as Indiska, H&M, IKEA, PUMA, and numerous others are setting high standards for their vendors that are improving the entire supply chain: from growing cotton and dying fabrics to manufacturing factories and distribution channels.

Indiska is a Swedish based retail company featuring clothing and products mainly from India and China with 90 stores in Sweden, Finland, and Norway, and has around 700 employees. They have a long history, dating back originally to 1901, with the current family ownership taking over in the fifties. They are very clear on the values of the organization and the way they do business through what they call their code of conduct. Because they are working with so many different suppliers in these developing countries, they have had challenges over the years that we have to say they've done an incredible job in influencing.

This company is a great example of working in collaboration with their partners. Over the years, they have been able to influence the working conditions of the factories, help to eliminate child labor, improve working hours and salaries, and become more environmentally friendly and aware throughout their entire production—even though they have not owned any of the factories themselves.

When we met with Renee Anderson, their head of ethics and environment, she shared how they have a long term perspective in their working relationships and made very deliberate

(continued)

efforts to improve their supply chain. She was able to influence factory owners to follow the established labor laws and give much better conditions from what had been the industry norm. In professionally requiring these changes of their suppliers, they have been able to better the lives of thousands of people.

Renee shared a great story with us. When she was first touring the factory of one of their bigger suppliers, the conditions were some of the worst she had seen. By the time they had finished the tour, the owner, Mr. Singh, and his wife were pale with fear and worry—they had no idea how they were going to fix the long list of issues they were supposed to deal with. Indiska was their biggest customer and they didn't want to lose their business. No one had ever enforced any of the changes that were now required (such as having separate and proper toilets for the women, wearing masks to avoid the inhalation of dust, making fire exits, fire training, paying for insurances and pension funds, etc.). Renee told them this should be made in a step-by-step improvement , giving them different time schedules to accomplish certain tasks with the expectation that the full list would be completed within a realistic timeline.

At the follow up meetings made by Renée, she was astounded at how quickly things had completely changed in this factory. It was like night and day. Apparently, once the Singh's and their management had started implementing the changes, they just kept right on going. When asked how he was able to make such drastic changes, Mr. Singh replied with a hearty laugh, he could tell her in three words: fear, awareness, and intent. The first was the paralyzing fear that they could lose their entire business if

(continued)

they lost Indiska as a customer. The second was the awareness of how poor the conditions actually were and that they were just being asked to follow the Indian labor laws (which had never been enforced). Last, was the intent that they wanted to be the best factory working for Indiska and that they would stay at number one. In fact, they've grown their business and gained several other large retail clients and have opened up additional factories—all with the high standards, providing great jobs and helping hundreds of families live in better conditions.

Although India is a huge country and the problems are immense, we can see how working together through business, you can collaborate and give back in a big way. It is a great example of making the world a better place by becoming aware and setting that intent.

Indiska is now working with 35 other retailers and with the Stockholm International Water Institute to improve the water supply throughout the textile industry with the Sweden Textile Water Initiative. This is yet another project that shows that we are gaining a great awareness in many industries about how we are using our natural resources.

We believe we can all learn from Mr. Singh's wise journey of going from fear to awareness to intent. We are leaving the competitive model and moving towards a collaborative model where we are working together for the good of humanity and our planet.

3. Thriving Culture

The culture of a company is an intangible yet undeniable part of a company. A Thriving Culture focuses on what is working, maximizes that, and, at the same time, eliminates what is not working.

A Thriving Culture is deliberate—a very conscious way of creating an environment where employees thrive and is reinforced by the processes, policies, and procedures. A Thriving Culture allows for creativity and innovation throughout the organization because the core values are clear and decisions can be made that are always aligned with those values first.

In a Thriving Culture, everyone is empowered. There is flexibility and scalability because people can make decisions that keep things moving forward based on the values and culture of the organization. It becomes much easier to avoid people, products, or processes that simply don't fit in or that undermine the core values of the culture.

You can get a sense of a company's culture just by walking through the environment.

If you take an established company, they tend to have all the systems and resources in place. You find a more structured environment, often with offices and cubicles. Often, there is a seriousness that is all about doing business and people need to stay within certain parameters. With a start-up company, the culture generally tends to be more chaotic. People are running around and job descriptions are blurry at best. Everyone chips in to get the job done, whatever that may be at that moment. Resources tend to be scarce, so there is a nervous energy, yet it's an exciting time of creation and innovation. We use those two extremes to point out the differences; however, these are the physical clues of the environment. Much of the culture of the company comes from the individuals that are working at the company.

In *Tribal Leadership,* authors Dave Logan, John King, and Halee Fischer-Wright discuss that people are naturally tribal in nature and that the maximum number of people in a tribe should be 150. There are companies that will strategically keep that level and just open new buildings with different departments as they grow to keep that feeling of tribal culture alive within the organization. Larger companies are made up of several tribes or departments; each has a bit of its own sub-culture.

W. L. Gore & Associates, Inc, an inspiring US company probably most known for its Gore-Tex fabric, and the fact that they have been included in FORTUNE's annual list of the U.S. "100 Best Companies to Work For" for sixteen consecutive years (including 2013 at the time of this writing and a distinction that only five companies have), is one company that has followed the magic number of 150. Bill Gore, the founder, came to realize that as a company grew over 150 employees, it was hard to know everyone's name. So he decided to cap all of his factories at 150 employees. This way the employees could all know each other by name and keep a sense of community and camaraderie with the group. It has been a strategy that has worked for them.

Robin Dunbar, a professor of evolutionary anthropology at the University of Oxford, has researched this idea so deeply, the number 150 has been dubbed "Dunbar's Number". He believes that human beings can hold only about 150 meaningful relationships in their heads. With the rise in use of technology to stay connected, Dunbar states that there are some neurological mechanisms in place to help us cope with the ever-growing amount of social connections life seems to require. Humans have the ability, for example, to facially recognize about 1,500 people.[52]

In a world that is expanding and advancing quickly, we seem to be driven by deeply-rooted feeling for community and connection, regardless what that magic number might be. Today's companies provide the opportunity to create our tribes.

One observation is that every single company that exists went through its infancy to toddler stages where everything was chaotic. But as organizations grow and become more successful, they mature, just as we grow into adulthood, and then things become more serious, systematized, and process oriented. Those things *are* good, but it seems that often a larger, more mature company can lose its soul in a sense. It forgets what it was like to first walk, to stand on its own— unless there is a conscious effort to keep their culture and values alive. Developing a Thriving Culture is having an awareness and keeping—or bringing back—that sense of excitement and fun on some level.

That entrepreneurial spirit is much like a toddler's spirit. They are determined to win, they'll do whatever it takes to get their way, they are committed to making it happen, and, even though it might be crazy stressful times, they are doing what they are doing because they are passionate about it and have their dream.

Many larger companies have created a Thriving Culture where "Intrapreneurs" (an employee of a large corporation with the freedom and financial support to create new products, services, systems, etc.) can flourish and create their own dreams under the umbrella of the organization. These are the forward thinking, fully engaged employees who have a purpose to improve or expand a part of the business. HCL considers themselves the world's largest startup with over 90,000 employees because they have learned to empower their employees by fostering an entrepreneurial culture where employees listen to customer needs, innovate, and deliver solutions in a way that strengthens their customer relations.

Life Cycle of Business

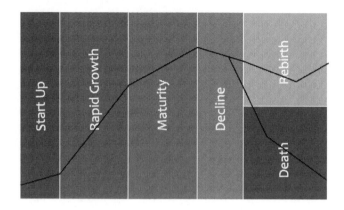

It is important to know at what state of growth and development the organization is in because it requires different skills and thinking to go to the next step. Any time you want to create change, you must identify your starting point and the destination. The path will not always be direct but, with those two points identified, you can begin to move forward on the path to growth and change.

One company that we are watching closely now is Nokia: the Finnish telecom giant that was on top of the market during the nineties but went into a fierce downward spiral after a few short years, starting in 2007. They made a crucial business error in deciding *not* to go into smart phones. Apple introduced the iPhone in 2007 and almost decimated one of Europe's most successful companies—and quickly. Just as Kodak fell from the top of its game, Nokia's fall has occurred, but in a much shorter span of time. If you look at the lifecycle chart, Nokia is at the precarious point of death or rebirth. From our research, we are hoping that Nokia can make a strong comeback through some sort of reinvention, and there are some signs of so. They are taking some interesting initiatives regarding recycling of mobile phones and the environment that are worth watching. Plus, this company has reinvented itself before so it is in their culture. But they have certainly paid a high price.

Here is another chart that can be helpful in describing your starting point.

Company Type & Leadership

	Start Up	Fast Growth		Maturation	Stagnation
Leadership Type	Planter	Builder		Change Agent	Super Change Agent
Climate	Frenetic Creative Fast Paced Exciting	Team Implementation Proactive Delegate	SWEET SPOT	Committees Continuity Organization Policies/Procedures	Committees Past Centered Crisis Survival
	Informal Opportunistic	Freedom Areas Vision/Direction		Status Quo Bureaucracy	Impersonal Turmoil
Result	Action	Growth/Change		Maintenance	Losses

Zappos has spent years working actively in developing their company culture. CEO Tony *Hsieh* shared in his book, *Delivering Happiness*, many of the strategies he has actively worked with to make Zappos one of The Most Amazing Companies.

According to Tony, the company culture and brand are two sides of the same coin—he states that "Your culture is your brand." Combining these two perspectives into one greater picture really ingrains the culture and the brand into everything everyone does and experiences with relation to the company—both internally and externally.

Tony continues to explain that brand, culture, and their employee development pipeline (BCP) are the three key areas Zappos focuses on to give them a competitive advantage. Everything else can and will be copied eventually.

Again, we return to transparency: would you be comfortable printing everything your employees, customers, and partners have to say about your culture? If not, what would it take to get there?

At HCL Technologies, the secret to their phenomenal growth during a global recession has been their philosophy that "Transparency is the new trust."

When your customers, employees, and partners are Raving Fans, transparency is a joy, not a threat!

At Southwest, culture is such a critical part of their success and performance, they have created a "culture committee", consisting of 96 employees that are nominated by their peers from all areas of the company. They are responsible for "doing whatever it takes to create, enhance, and enrich the special Southwest spirit and culture that has made it such a wonderful company/family".[53]

Taking time to define and nurture the culture of your company is truly one of the most essential steps along the journey to becoming amazing. It is where the employees will have the opportunity to be the best that they can be and your customers will receive incredible service and experience that will naturally grow the business.

The Thriving Culture is where the Raving Fans are born and bred!

■ Employees want to stay because they love the culture

Matching a personality to a culture is essential for long term employment and stability within an organization. Employees stay at a company that they enjoy working at longer. Whenever you have a group of people coming together for a shared purpose (i.e., children in need), a culture will emerge just from having the mix of those people. Culture is defined both tangibly and intangibly. The tangible aspects are the physical environment— are there cubicles and closed doors? Or an open plan with no set work spaces? How is it decorated—conservatively, modernly, rustic? What is the dress code, whether it's actually defined or not? Bankers and insurance tend to have suits, IT and media companies are generally much more casual.

The physical environment says a lot about the culture and smart companies invest in creating a pleasant and fun environment that people want to be in. If a company creates an environment that people really enjoy and want to hang out in, then clearly you'll have more productivity and creativity within the workplace. This is why Mircrosoft Sweden surveyed Millenniums (the Y Generation born between 1977-1997) and decided to totally remodel their offices specifically to make them more attractive to the millennial workforce. Patagonia receives 10,000 resumes for about 100 positions available because they offer employees an ideal way to integrate their home and their professional and recreational lives. They have on-site childcare and offer only local, organic foods in their cafeteria where it is common to see parents eating meals with their children.

There are also intangible aspects such as the reporting processes— are people afraid to speak up? What happens if someone makes a mistake? Can a person create their dream job within the company? How can someone grow and develop within the organization?

It is essential to fully understand both the tangible and intangible aspects of the culture and to look for ways to define, improve, and evolve a Thriving Culture that people want to be a part of— to be engaged in! It's great for both attraction *and* retention of great employees.

■ Make work FUN

One of the reasons Virgin has many long term employees is because they have fun. When people can laugh together and enjoy hanging out, there is a natural bonding that happens. The group grows to support each other, they can discuss their problems, and they can lean on each other during the tougher times. When they can have fun together, they create memories that can carry them through the challenging days if they arise. It just creates an environment where people want to be around each other.

Electrawinds, a Belgium alternative energy company, and one of our Most Amazing Company models, is very active in promoting fun activities for their employees, from community involvement to local sporting events. They have seen the added benefits their employees get by participating in these events; besides promoting health and wellbeing through physical activity for the employees and brand recognition at the events from the group outfits and sponsoring, they see their employees getting to know each other on deeper levels, which have improved communications and relationships within the company. So much so that the employees have initiated their own group activities and spend time going on annual ski trips together.

John Lewis is another example where they encourage their employees to be involved in fun activities and hobbies together. For example, there are several employee groups that will spend time following their passions such as surfing or biking. The employees from different departments learn more about each other because they have at least two things in common: they are working for the same company and are passionate about their hobbies. Again, the employees have fun together, often outside of their work hours, and develop bonds which strengthen their working relationships with people in other departments.

Many employees and management do *not* think of work as fun. Having fun at work can be a very foreign concept because we need to take things seriously all the time. Having the appropriate levels of fun will help your business grow. What sixty year-olds consider fun will most likely vary quite a bit from the twenty-somethings and a balance must be found. But it can be found! As with all things, the answers begin from within. And if someone is not used to having fun, they'll need to figure out what they consider fun.

Many of these Amazing Companies have CEOs that are quite playful. They can be found dressing up in crazy outfits, playing jokes either on the employees or customers, and dancing Gangnam Style or the Harlem Shake. Both Southwest and Virgin customers have experienced the infamous CEOs serving drinks on an occasional flight.

We are spending roughly one third of our lives at work so why should anyone dread it? In general, it's time to lighten up at work and create a fun place to be.

■ Collaboration (Teamwork)

Teamwork is something that companies have worked on for years. Collaboration is taking it to the next level because there is a clearly defined purpose and vision everyone is working towards. With teamwork, you still can create the "us and them" mentality, where it's competitive and comparing instead of focused on the bigger purpose for existing in the first place.

A recent McKinsey study tried to measure the benefits of collaboration. Their global institute believes you can generate a ROI from Web 2.0 and social media, and they back this up by saying that companies that adopt web technology tools are market leaders and have larger market shares and higher product margins.[54]

McKinsey calls this new class of companies the "Networked Enterprise".

Many years ago, Dr. Nick Bontis at McMaster University in Canada showed that there was a high correlation between the use of collaboration tools and a slower rate of employee turnover.[55] McKinsey, in their recent report, have also identified benefits, as well as noting their popularity within the sampled population.[56]

- 77% Increased Access to knowledge
- 60% Reduced Communication Costs
- 52% Increased speed of Access to Internal Experts (expertise discovery)
- 44% decreased travel costs
- 41% Increased employee satisfaction
- 40% Reduced operational Costs
- 29% Reduced time to Market for Products
- 28% Increases Innovation
- 18% Increased Revenue

Collaboration is more than just working together; there is a deeper level of support and commitment to each other to be successful. Each party has a vested interest in seeing the other succeed—and they celebrate it! They are happy for each other because they know it's for the greater good of the whole.

Collaboration fosters a "we" mentality, and there isn't a focus on the individual. The focus is on the group and the higher mission to accomplish. An important component to this is also celebration, which we'll discuss in more detail shortly, and it is here that the individual, the group, and the organization are all acknowledged.

A Thriving Culture is created from a shared bigger purpose and aligned values that each individual believes in wholeheartedly. It raises an organization to a greater level of service in the world, a place that each employee is excited to be a part of and contributing to. A Thriving Culture becomes your family away from home because of the deeply shared beliefs in what you are doing.

Because we spend so much of our waking hours at work, just imagine being able to love what you are doing, feel like you are contributing significantly, sense an excitement for spending time with your coworkers and team members, and know that you are making a difference in the world. And that the positive energy you get at work spills into the other areas of your life so that you are living a balanced and fulfilling—and let's not forget fun!—life where your relationships are great, you feel wonderful, and you are accomplishing all that you want in your life. This is not a fantasy! The great news is that this can be your reality and just by being open to all these concepts, you are already on your way to achieving this state of being!

11

Productivity

Productivity is a result. When your organization is productive, it means the people are engaged, thriving and are able to perform at high levels. The company is energized, enthused, and has a clear vision of what they need to do to get where you all want to go. The steps are clear and people are all contributing to make it happen.

When a company has gotten clear on the true purpose, and has ignited the passion for that shared vision, the people step up to the plate and make it happen. Our 6P's model has a domino effect. Once you get the foundational pieces in place, then the fun can really start.

Being productive is not only great for the company, it's good for each individual to feel like they are moving forward, reaching their goals and targets, and playing an important part of the overall game.

High productivity comes from having the right leaders creating the right environment that allows employees to thrive and to feel empowered.

In this section, we'll look at building up the house through Dynamic Leadership and Visionary Leaders within the organization and at the importance of creating Trust and Freedom, all of which foster a highly productive organization.

1. Dynamic Leadership

Dynamic Leadership allows natural leaders to rise up and lead by example. This is not only for executive management. It is for anyone who can lead the way to improvements and positive change. It is a way of transforming the organization by focusing efforts on what is needed to make people more effective.

- Take some time to think about what in your company enables people to work at their best and what doesn't. The obstacles are likely to be rigid rules and procedures, levels of approval, and micromanagement in general.
- Dynamic leadership is forward thinking but it also is keeping everyone on the boat working at their best. **Moving from an authoritative type of culture to one of believing the best of everyone and making the people feel valued is transformative for an organization.**

The key to effective change: Empower; don't dictate

Dynamic leaders ask the person whether they genuinely want to facilitate whatever change is needed or whether they have a specific solution they want to put in place. By taking the time to listen to the input from front line staff, it shows there is a vested interest and will increase loyalty when employees know they have a say in the matter. The point is, the most resistant employees will welcome change when they have been involved in creating it.

■ Empowers people

Many of our corporations, and certainly the industrial based models, have created a culture driven by hierarchy and fear.

No one feels good at work when they are walking around on eggshells, wondering when they will be yelled at the next time, or if they are insecure that they might be fired, or even in an environment where gossip pervades and backstabbing and climbing the corporate ladder at all costs is the norm. Why would anyone want to work there? Do you work best when shouted at? Or when supported and made to feel good? In working with many entrepreneurs over the years, we started to hear over and over with a huge sign of relief, "oh, I escaped the corporate world." Why should people feel imprisoned by their jobs? Isn't an empowering culture much more effective? Our research and numerous studies show hands down this is true.

Leaders must live the values by example. A company that is driven by fear or greed will often create an environment of distrust and denigration. When you have leadership that is supportive and collaborative, you empower the people to excel and grow. True dynamic leadership fuels the vision of the company, rallies the troops, brings enthusiasm and energy to the mission, and encourages the employees to reach success.

Again, we come back to "the power within an organization is truly in its people." This is what makes the creation of the products and services possible. Even the support staff plays a very important part. It is a system that requires all the parts to work together in unison. And when everyone knows the full picture and how important their role is—a role they may have earlier thought didn't really make a difference—then the results will grow and the business will find its flow. The business will be on the upward spiral to success.

■ Bringing out the best in people

Dynamic leaders understand that the human capital of the company is its biggest asset, and they know how to bring out the best in each person. They allow growth and development, they look for the talents and passions of individuals, and put those individuals in positions where they can fully utilize those for the best of the individual and the company. When you focus on the talents, you will allow your greatness to shine through. There is a superhero within each and every one of us!

Not everyone is meant to be a leader. Some people do not want to step into that role, and that is perfectly okay. The same is true in the management role. It is also important to understand that just because a salesperson hits their targets does not mean they should naturally be promoted to a sales manager. Too often someone is following a career path that takes them away from their passions and talents and puts them into something they do not want to be doing. But to step down from that looks like a career dead end.

We need to allow people to follow their passions and then find or create jobs and tasks around their strengths in order to excel. A talented leader knows how to do this. Dynamic leaders know how to spot the best and bring that to the forefront.

There was a very successful CEO of a garment company in Los Angeles who intuitively allowed his employees to follow their passions. When he saw that someone was really happy with a different task than what was in their official job description, he quickly changed their job to focus on the task that was making them happy and hired another person for the other job. Turnover is historically quite high in this industry, yet the turnover with this company was comparatively low and those who left often came back within a year or two, wanting to return. This leader knew how to take care of employees and it paid off many times over for him.

There must also be allowance for people who are not in your typical leadership role to feel empowered to make a difference in the company. A receptionist who worked at a busy advertising agency understood that even though she was "just the receptionist", she was most often the first point of contact with their clients. So her phone mannerisms shined through with customer service and friendliness that made all the clients feel special. She asked the owner of the agency if she could buy fresh flowers for the reception area and always made sure it was inviting. Clients began to comment on how pleasant it was to interact with her, and soon her enthusiasm began to spread into the organization.

Dynamic leaders are the people who lead by example to make a big difference in a company and know instinctively how to bring out the best in people.

They also understand the power of collaboration and working together to create value. The reason we like the word collaboration so much is that it is the next level of evolution. There is a genuine caring underlying a collaborative effort. Although not everyone is meant to be a leader of people, everyone should definitely be made to feel they are an important part of the team and that's where dynamic leadership comes in. If everyone can look at their role and tasks and see how they can improve them for the good of the group, then they feel empowered all the while contributing to the bigger goals as well.

CHARACTERISTICS OF EFFECTIVE TEAMS

- Clear sense of purpose and goals
- Team gets things done
- Individuals understand their responsibilities/ carry their own weight
- Members experience a sense of belonging to the team
- High levels of trust among team members
- Comfortable atmosphere; team members care for each other
- Conflict is dealt with openly
- Everyone participates in discussions
- Group is not dominated by a few individuals
- People are free in expressing feelings and ideas
- People listen to each other
- Decisions are made when there is general agreement

We wanted to share a wonderful story about how anyone can make a difference and epitomized the concept of Dynamic Leaders. Barbara Glanz tells the story best in her own words.[57]

JOHNNY THE BAGGER® – by Barbara Glanz

I am an author and a professional speaker. I travel all over the world speaking on the topics of Employee Engagement, Customer Service, Spreading Contagious Enthusiasm™ and Change. Several years ago I was asked to speak to 3000 employees of a large supermarket chain, an experience which led to one of the most heartwarming blessings of my entire speaking career.

Recently in my presentations I have been focusing on the idea of "Adding a Personal Signature to your Work." With all the downsizing, re-engineering, overwhelming technological changes, and stress, I think it is essential for each of us to find a way we can really feel good about ourselves and our jobs, and one of the most powerful ways to do this is to do something that differentiates you from all the other people who do the same thing you do.

Some of the examples I share are a United airlines pilot who, after everything is under control in the cockpit, goes to the computer and at random selects several people on board the flight and handwrites them a thank you note for their business. A graphic artist I work with always encloses a piece of sugarless gum in everything he sends his customers, so you never throw anything from him away! A Northwest Airlines baggage attendant decided that his personal signature would be to collect all the luggage tags that fall off customer's suitcases, which in the past have been simply tossed in the garbage, and in his free time he sends them back with a note thanking them for flying Northwest. A senior manager with whom I worked decided that his personal signature would be that

(continued)

152

whenever he sends his employees a memo with news that he knows they won't like very much, he staples a piece of kleenex to the corner of the memo!

After sharing several other examples of how people add their unique spirit to their jobs, my challenge to them is to get their creative juices going to come up with their OWN creative personal signature. Since I am also a writer, I always give my home telephone number to everyone in the audience, encouraging them to call me and let me know what they have decided to do so that I can share it with others in my speaking and writing.

About 3 weeks after I had spoken to the supermarket employees, my phone rang late one afternoon. The person on the line told me that his name was Johnny and that he was a bagger in one of the stores. He also told me that he was a person of Down Syndrome. He said, "Barbara, I liked what you said!" Then he went on to tell me how when he'd gone home that night, he asked his Dad to teach him to use the computer.

He said they set it up in three columns, and each night when he goes home, he finds a "thought for the day." He said, "If I can't find one I like, I think one up!" Then he and his Dad type it into the computer, six times on a page, and they print out at least 50 pages each night. Then he cuts them out, signs his name on the back of each one, and the next day "with flourish," **he puts a thought for the day in each person's groceries he bags**, adding his own personal signature in a heartwarming, fun, and creative way.

(continued)

One month later the manager of the store called me. He said, "Barbara, you won't believe what happened today. . . . . When I went out on the floor this morning, the line at Johnny's checkout was *three times longer* than any other line!" He said, "I went ballistic, yelling, 'Get more lanes open! Get more people out here,' but the customers said, 'No no! We *want* to be in Johnny's lane — we want the thought for the day!' "

He said one woman even came up and told him, "I only used to shop once a week, and now I come in every time I go by because I want the thought for the day!" (Imagine what that does to the bottom line . . . .) He ended by saying, "Who do you think is the **most important person** in our whole store?" Johnny, of course!

Three months later he called me again, "You and Johnny have transformed our store! Now in the floral department when they have a broken flower or an unused corsage, they go out on the floor and find an elderly woman or a little girl and pin it on them. One of our meat packers loves Snoopy, so he bought 50,000 Snoopy stickers, and each time he packages a piece of meat, he puts a Snoopy sticker on it. **We** are having so much fun, and our **customers** are having so much fun!" THAT is spirit in the workplace!

It never ceases to amaze me, whenever I tell this beautiful story, how little it takes to regenerate the spirit in a workplace. Johnny took what many of us might consider to be a not very important job and he made it important by adding his own personal signature. My challenge and yours – *if Johnny can do it, there is no reason why each one*

(continued)

> *of us can't do it, too.* Imagine the new spirit of self-esteem, commitment, and fun which could permeate our places of work if we each, like Johnny, found a way to add our special, unique touch to our job!
>
> This story is excerpted from the following books: *CARE Packages for the Workplace — Dozens of Little Things You Can Do to Regenerate Spirit at Work,* Barbara A. Glanz, 1996; *CARE Packages for the Home—Dozens of Ways to Regenerate Spirit Where You Live,* Barbara A. Glanz 1998; and *The Simple Truths of Service Inspired by Johnny the Bagger,* Ken Blanchard and Barbara Glanz, 2005. © Barbara Glanz Communications, Inc., 2005. All rights reserved.
>

■ Allows creativity and innovation to flourish

By allowing people to follow their passions, identify their talents, and to focus their efforts in those areas, it will open up an individual to reaching their full potential. It promotes creativity and innovation. Employees will flourish and grow. A company will benefit hugely by allowing creativity to flow. The answers to problems can easily come from within when asked. But if the employees are not asked, they do not feel valued and they then develop an attitude of just doing their job, nothing more. But when their opinions are asked for, are listened to, and are acted upon, it raises their level of confidence, makes them feel more loyalty, allows them to contribute, and makes them want to do more.

Dynamic leaders foster a culture and environment of creativity and innovation that will propel the company forward. Business has typically been very analytical and rational. By allowing time for creative thought processes, it can open up entirely new avenues that wouldn't have been explored otherwise. We will discuss some examples in more detail in the Trust & Freedom section.

Dynamic Leaders, whether they are in a management role or not, have three main jobs:

1. They are able to communicate a vision so that it inspires others. This is often through verbal and/or communication. But the underlying actions are what truly support their vision. Are they really walking the talk?

2. They live the values of the organization. Again, their actions must support what they are saying. This is why doing the work on the values is instrumental to shifting an organization in significant ways.

3. They are able to manage the emotional states of others. This is where their true and natural talents come into play. They can inspire and motivate others, thereby causing positive actions and results from the group that move the organization and its mission forward.

2. Visionary Leaders

"Practice Golden Rule#1 of Management in everything you do. Manage others the way you would like to be managed."
— *Brian Tracy*

The journey to a fully engaged organization, a Most Amazing Company, must start with the leadership being open to empowering the employees. If the executives do not embrace these ideas, the desired outcome will not be attained.

Visionary leaders are those who are open minded, humble, down to earth in how they interact with people. Yet they also tend to be driven, goal oriented, focused on results, and hold a clear picture on where they are taking the organization. Ultimately, it is people who engage people so leaders play a pivotal role in the engagement of an organization.

■ Leaders inspire others to discover their greatness

Visionary leaders are here to support employees and to allow others to flourish and thrive. They are supportive and see the greatness and potential in people. They are forgiving and allow mistakes, as long as someone learns from it.

These leaders have eliminated a fear driven environment. They hold the vision of greatness not only for the company but also for each of the employees. They are able to empower and develop employees to be fully engaged. They see the value the company brings to the market, and are always looking to improve and move the company forward.

Google conducted some interesting research, called Project Oxygen, with a mission to build better bosses. In a culture of engineers, the tendency is to leave them alone and to let them do their work. What they found was that people did want inter-action with their supervisors, but in a non-imposing manner. "What employees valued most were even-keeled bosses who made time for one-on-one meetings, who helped people puzzle through problems by asking questions, not dictating answers, and who took an interest in employees' lives and careers."[58] Again, the connection, the human connection is essential, particularly for managers and leaders.

Daniel Goleman, author of the highly acclaimed *Emotional Intel-ligence,* has found in his research that the best leaders have a high level of emotional intelligence. The five areas in which they

157

excelled were self-awareness, self-regulation, motivation, empathy, and social skill. The following chart shows a summary of what each entails.[59]

5 Components of Emotional Intelligence at Work

	DEFINITION	HALLMARKS
Self-Awareness	The ability to recognize and understand your moods, emotions, and drives, as well as their effect on others	Self-confidence, realistic self-assessment, self-deprecating sense of humor
Self-Regulation	The ability to control or redirect disruptive impulses and moods The propensity to suspend judgment – to think before acting	Trustworthiness and integrity Comfort with ambiguity Openness to change
Motivation	A passion to work for reasons that go beyond money or status A propensity to pursue goals with energy and persistence	Strong drive to achieve Optimism, even in the face of failure Organizational commitment
Empathy	The ability to understand the emotional makeup of other people Skill in treating people according to their emotional reactions	Expertise in building and retaining talent Cross-cultural sensitivity Service to clients and customers
Social Skill	Proficiency in managing relationships and building networks An ability to find common ground and build rapport	Effectiveness in leading change Persuasiveness Expertise in building and leading teams

Emotional intelligence is recognized as a desirable quality for leaders to have because they simply make better leaders. It is said that a leadership style will determine close to 70 percent of the emotional climate, which drives 20-30 percent of business performance.[60] They can connect and relate to people on a deeper level, often coming from their heart. Leaders who aren't afraid to show that they love people and their work get others to follow them easily.

We interviewed Sweden's Manager of the Year for 2012, Lars Kry, CEO of Proffice, to get his insights into leadership. He has seen much success in growing Proffice because of his ability to delegate and empower his teams. He believes there are four key factors to great leadership:

1. 100 percent agreement—get everyone on board and in full understanding. This significantly decreases time wasted with misunderstandings and miscommunication. (The consensus leadership style is quite strong in the Nordic countries and, although many say it slows down the decision making process, it is inclusive and makes employees feel their opinions are valuable.)

2. Tools—make sure that everyone has the tools needed to do their jobs well.

3. Be the best at what you do—match talents well to their job duties and then allow people to excel at what they do best.

4. Feedback—giving feedback is essential for employees to know they are on track. Giving feedback often helps to keep the business progressing on course.

What is rising to the forefront as well now is the authenticity of the leaders. Are they being true not only to themselves but to the world in how they present themselves?

In one of our own mastermind groups, an individual shared that he refused to do business with a well known company simply because he found out the founder and management went on a shooting safari in Africa during a trip. It was so out of alignment with his values, that was the kiss of death of a long standing customer—and the sad thing is that these leaders probably have no idea. Yet they have a disgruntled customer that is spreading his opinions on this.

As a leader, it means being aware of all of your actions and taking responsibility for them—especially in our transparent world. We have seen countless examples of poor judgment and leadership that can destroy year's worth of brand building just through a misguided statement or action.

The visionary leader understands that the greatness of the organization is a team effort, and, in inspiring this, they cultivate their own excellence as a leader as well. The focus, however, is always on the group efforts and the vision of the company.

■ Hold a clear vision

We had an interesting conversation with a chairman of the board for several large global companies. His background was finance, operations, and private equity, but he also understood the importance of cultural development. He asked, "What do you think comes first: the profits or the culture?" We got into an interesting discussion because in his mind, the profits had to come in order to invest in the company and that came about from the visionary leadership. We countered that it all starts with the visionary entrepreneur who inspires others to help create and develop a company.

Today's entrepreneurs have this different mindset to build their company through engaging their employees and creating an amazing culture. And many, like Blake McCoskie, are building the giving back into their business models, which helps to create the culture and deep value connection for employees and customers alike.

These leaders understand that the big picture is essential to reach. They are able to inspire and motivate others to accomplish what needs to be done to achieve their vision. Every decision they make is with this big vision in mind and that gives them the clarity to give them confidence and direction not only for themselves but for the whole organization, too.

There is more than just lip service to the mission of the company, something that often occurs. They provide the laser focus to accomplish the goals and are able to inspire others to stay on course with that objective. They are like the captain of the boat who is able to guide the ship to safety through the storms and night skies because they know the final destination and stay on course to get there.

In recent years, we've seen one scandal after another in the business world. It is, unfortunately, that a few misguided leaders can truly damage solid brands. Often, you find there is a small core group who has a hidden agenda that benefits them directly, many times at the cost of the employees or the true purpose of the company. It is essential to weed out these people because it takes a long time to restore brand trust.

The good news is that because of our transparent world, these discrepancies are coming to light to be changed. But it would be best to avoid those situations in the first place by engaging leadership that has integrity, vision, and values that benefit the organization, its employees, and its customers.

■ Excellent communicators

Visionary Leaders are able to convey the vision and message both within the company and to the market. They are not afraid to face the public and tend to be very charismatic individuals who attract others to follow them. They are not afraid to admit mistakes and are able to move forward quickly from any sort of setbacks. They see the lessons from any mistakes and are able to take the value from that lesson to make improvements. They can paint the vision of the future and get others to believe that it is not only possible; it is also attainable by them.

We find that successful leadership is shifting. The more caring and inspiring, the more effective leaders can be.[61]

The 7 key aspects of leadership for the next decade
1. Vision
2. Courage
3. Integrity
4. Caring
5. Strategic Planning
6. Focus
7. Inspiration & collaboration

According to a survey by Gallup, the best leaders are those who give recognition on a weekly basis. People have a need to know how they are doing, and, because of the world of instant gratification we're living in now with Facebook likes and twitter followers, we need to hear that we're on the right track. This is something that has been researched extensively in the gaming industry. People playing games are so engaged specifically because they are getting constant feedback, and are able to course correct, while getting recognition for their accomplishments, both small and large.

So being an excellent communicator and giving feedback is essential in these times to inspire the best of the employees.

■ The difference between a manager and a leader

We believe there is a distinct difference between a leader and a manager. A leader is someone who can inspire others to take action and holds the vision for what is possible. They drive the organization forward from a *visionary perspective*. Leaders inspire trust in people and innovate to drive the group forward. They have a very high emotional intelligence and can relate very well to people on many levels.

A manager is someone who is overseeing tasks that need to be accomplished. They are driving an organization forward from an *operational perspective*. Managers rely on control and administer tasks to maintain the group. Since they are managing a group of people focusing on getting tasks done, they, too, need a high level of emotional intelligence.

The manner in which leaders and managers do their work is very different. And often they are confused. A person can be a good leader but a horrible manager, and vice versa. It is a matter of knowing a person's strengths and talents so that they are matched with the right position.

| The Difference Between a Boss and a Leader ||
Boss	Leader
Drives employees	Coaches employees
Inspires fear	Generates enthusiasm
Places blame for problems & breakdowns	Finds solutions & fixes breakdowns
Knows how it is done	Shows how it is done
Uses people	Develops people
Takes credit	Gives credit
Demands	Asks
Says "go"	Says "let's go"

> Leading is not the same as being a leader. Leading means others are willing to follow not because they have to, but because they want to. — *Simon Sinek*

We believe that in today's economy, we need more leaders. We need heroes that make conscious decisions to do business in a different way; to use business as a force for good.

Advice from Richard Branson:

Find people smarter than you and make them see their work as a MISSION!

In a blog post by Vishen Lakhiani, founder of Mind Valley, he tells the story of a discussion he had with Sir Richard Branson. Vishen writes:

So while having dinner with Sir Richard Branson on Necker Island, his private hangout in the British Virgin Islands, I finally got to ask him a question I've always wanted to ask.

We had been talking about life, fatherhood, kids, spiritual ideas, business and more. And I finally asked him...

"Richard, there has been so many theories about what makes you tick. I mean the 300+ companies, taking man to space, and all the other crazy epic things you do. But if YOU had to boil it down to ONE thing. Just one thing. What would your advice be?"

And this is what Branson told me. (Note that I'm paraphrasing a bit, because I did not record this.)

"It's all about finding and hiring people smarter than you. Getting them to join your business. And giving them good work. Then getting out of their way. And trusting them. You have to get out of the way so YOU can focus on the bigger vision. That's important. And here's the main thing... you must make them see their work as a MISSION."

JUST DO IT!
- Believe it can be done
- Have goals
- Prepare well
- Help each other

HAVE FUN
- Have fun, work hard, and the money will come
- Don't waste time—grab your chances
- Have a positive outlook on life
- When it's not fun, move on

BE BOLD
- Calculate the risks and take them
- Believe in yourself
- Chase your dreams
- Have no regrets
- Be Bold
- Keep your word

CHALLENGE YOURSELF
- Aim high
- Try new things
- Always try
- Challenge yourself

STAND ON YOUR OWN FEET
- Rely on yourself
- Chase your dreams but live in the real world
- Work together

LIVE THE MOMENT
- Love life and live it to the full
- Enjoy the moment
- Reflect on your life
- Make every second Count
- Don't have regrets

VALUE FAMILY AND FRIENDS
- Put the family and fam first
- Be loyal
- Face problems head on
- Money is for making things happen
- Pick the right people and reward talent

HAVE RESPECT
- Be polite and respectful
- Do the right thing
- Keep your good name
- Be fair in all your dealings

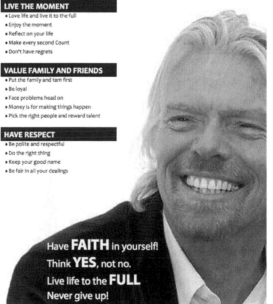

Have **FAITH** in yourself!
Think **YES**, not no.
Live life to the **FULL**
Never give up!

Trust & Freedom

> "A company is much stronger if it is bound by love rather than fear." — *Herb Kelleher, cofounder of Southwest Airlines*

Employees are more productive, creative, and responsible when given the freedom to do their jobs. We no longer live in times where people need hand holding or need to be micro managed. Employees are hired to do a certain job and managers need to get out of their way. A manager's role is there more to support and give guidelines... then allow the employees to excel at their jobs.

Richard Branson shares in his book, *Screw Business As Usual,* that one of his success strategies is to "inspire people to think like entrepreneurs, and whatever you do, treat them like adults. The hardest taskmaster of all is a person's own conscience, so the more responsibility you give people, the better they will work for you."[62]

In the *Happiness Manifesto*, Henry Steward discusses an empowering concept of how pre-approval has a very positive effect on a company culture. This is when a manager gives a task or objective to be completed and pre-approves the way in which it is completed. It gives the employees full control over achieving the results in the way that they think is best. It encourages people to take more ownership and responsibility for their work. This also encourages innovation and creates a culture of looking for solutions. It has an overall positive effect on reaching goals and accomplishing tasks.

When the values are aligned in the organization, it will naturally guide the employees to do what is best for the company according to the shared value system. Therefore, it becomes a win-win-win for everyone. It makes it easier for the manager to trust and get out of the way, it puts the responsibility on the employee making them feel more in control and able to contribute in more significant ways, and the results can often be new innovative means that might not have otherwise come up because it releases creativity and new ways of thinking.

■ Autonomy and mastery

Mastery is allowing someone to follow their passions and interests to become an expert in a certain area. When you allow the freedom to pursue what someone loves to do, you get a higher level of productivity and engagement.

Daniel Pink, author of the NY Times best-selling book *Drive,* talks about the science of motivation and a new business model that focuses on autonomy, mastery, and purpose.[63] Autonomy is the ability to work on our own, urge to direct our own lives. Mastery is the desire to get better and better at something that matters. And purpose is the yearning to do what we do in the service of something larger than ourselves. He describes these three elements as the building blocks for a new way of doing things. He explains that more engagement and more self direction work better.

There are numerous examples of companies that allow free thinking and creativity which has resulted in real bottom line benefits for an organization. Google is known for their innovative freedoms that they give to their employees. One such initiative is what they call "20 percent time" where employees can work on anything they want during that time. Half of their new products in a typical year are birthed during this 20 percent time—innovations such as Gmail and Google news originated from teams of employees thinking outside of their typical job descriptions.

Another company that is giving their employees more autonomy to determine their work is Atlassian, an Australian software company that gives all employees 24 hours each quarter to work on anything they want. They call these "ShipIt Days" because, like

FedEx, you have to deliver something overnight. Then they have a party to present what they have worked on and everyone votes on the best innovation. They have developed a whole array of software fixes from these internal events. Many companies are following suit with this and even high schools are beginning to adopt this new way of creativity and fun that inspires employees.

Philips also had a similar project called Accelerate Days in the Nordic region. The entire company spent a couple of days brainstorming new ideas that were submitted to a team. Over three hundred innovative ideas surfaced and they narrowed them down to thirty, which they then voted on within the organization to implement and have taken them in order of priority. Again, organizations are beginning to tap into the incredible resources they have within their companies—there is a lot of untapped potential sitting in the minds of the employees and figuring out a way to access it helps a company be innovative and grow. Plus it gives the employees the confirmation that they are indeed valued!

For years, new employees at Nordstrom's were given a copy of the Nordstrom's Employee Handbook—a single 5-by-8-inch gray card containing 75 words:

Welcome to Nordstrom

We're glad to have you with our company. Our number one goal is to provide outstanding customer service. Set both your personal and professional goals high. We have great confidence in your ability to achieve them.

Nordstrom Rules: Rule#1: Use best judgment in all situations. There will be no additional rules.

Please feel free to ask your department manager, store manager, or division general manager any question at any time.

Today, new hire orientations provide reading only the words "Use good judgment," supplemented by handbook of other general legal regulations and company expectations. However, using one's best judgment remains Nordstrom employees' number one policy in all aspects of the job.[64]

■ ROWE—Results-Oriented Work Environment

Focus on results and trust your people to find the best ways for *them* to get those results. Then just get out of their way. How many employees feel meetings are a productive use of their time? One of the common complaints you hear from company employees is the number of meetings they are required to attend and how much time is wasted there. Give people the freedom to manage their time wisely and if you are clear on the results or outcome you wish to see, then allow them to drive that process forward.

Results-Only Work Environment is a management strategy where employees are evaluated on performance, not presence. The focus is on results and only results—increasing the organization's performance while creating the right climate for people to manage all the demands in their lives including work. There are no schedules and people have full autonomy. How they get their work done, when, and where, are all up to the individuals. Meetings are optional and pre-agreed upon by the team. The results from this strategy are simple:

- Productivity goes up
- Worker engagement goes up
- Worker satisfaction goes up
- Employee turnover goes down

Daniel Pink also discusses extrinsic versus intrinsic motivation. Our business world is built around extrinsic motivators, reward/

punishment incentives that are not as effective as they once were thought to be. Today's workers are more motivated by intrinsic motivators—things that matter to them. It comes down to the values again and being aware of what they are and how to align with them.

Wikipedia is a prime example of allowing a great service to be built by giving access to people who are passionate about what they do. It has been built 100 percent by volunteers and is a great resource available to everyone. We believe we will see more and more of these types of services emerging as people allow their hobbies to reach a global market via the Internet.

■ Flexibility in the workplace

There is no denying that companies that allow more flexibility keep their employees happier and retention is higher. Rigidness of work hours, dress code, and the ability to get a job done in a certain way are falling to the wayside in light of looking at employee satisfaction. A company needs to allow the employees to be responsible and integrate their life/work balance in a way that works best for all parties. Flexibility is a way of keeping your employees happy—as long as they are held accountable for well defined results.

The ability to have a flexible schedule in our demanding lives is essential to keeping it all together. For example, with parents, it is of great importance to focus our children and employers who allow parents to work around their activities are doing a service by helping the employees feel they are able to contribute to their family *and* to their company without compromising either one. Plus, with the connectedness of technology, we really don't need to be tied to a desk or office any longer.

Sweden is quite progressive in this area. The social system allows for parents of young children to take significant time off for maternity leave (for both the mothers and fathers) but then also give the support with the daycare system to return to work easily. Companies in Sweden are generally very flexible in allowing parents to take time to be with their children during important school activities, which of course, leads to happier employees since they are able to be there for their children.

Expect to see a rise in the relevance globally of more progressive programs concerning workplace wellness, work-life balance, re-skilling, mentoring, employee satisfaction, flexibility, telecommuting, and other initiatives as the importance of the human capital outlook takes hold.

In *Tribal Leadership*, different levels of development for organizations are defined. A stage three company has an environment of "I'm great" where the individual strives alone to succeed and accomplish what he or she sets out to do. In this culture, trust must be earned. When an organization evolves to state four, the purpose and reason for existing becomes bigger than the individual and a "we're great" environment emerges. It is an environment of collaboration. Trust is not something to be earned but rather, the relationships start on the basis of trust already existing.

Managers who have learned to manage by being in control will have a lot of resistance to this. They must understand that their role is not to oversee all the details but to support and coach others to their own greatness. In order to do this, they must be willing to allow more freedom and empower others to take control and drive projects forward. Once they can see that the results and the benefits are greater using this model, it becomes easier for them to adapt and evolve to new levels as well.

In Whole Foods, they understand the importance of trust as they openly talk about it on their website. In their Declaration of Interdependence, they strive to:

"Instill a clear sense of interdependence among our various stakeholders (the people who are interested and benefit from the success of our company) is contingent upon our efforts to communicate more often, more openly, and more compassionately. Better communication equals better understanding and more trust."[65]

In today's business world, trust is essential. Flexibility and speed are much more valuable qualities than the tradition strategies and analysis we've been using for so long. These qualities force the organizations to take on responsibilities and actions in a timely manner. Because changes are happening so quickly, we need a high degree of resiliency and ability to adapt quickly in order to stay in the game. An organization that is run by control or fear will never be able to make the necessary changes in the short time needed. You need to have empowered employees that can make decisions and take action. To have that, there needs to be a high degree of trust and freedom.

12

Profits

In all of our work, we are certainly advocates of making a profit and bringing shareholder value. The company must be profitable in order to exist. Many of the problems we have today are the complete and utter focus on *only* making profits, even to the detriment of many other factors such as employee wellbeing, the environment, the lack of integrity, etc.

A company does not exist solely for the purpose of making a profit. There are probably many people that will disagree with this statement. That is only because we've been conditioned to think this way. Amazing Companies are most often driven by human behavior, while Wall Street analysts have a much easier time understanding a numbers-based business model. It is a belief system we have in many of our societies and cultures... and it is time to upgrade those outdated beliefs. "We readily talk about the value of a company's intellectual property; why not take its emotional property into account when assessing its investment value?"[66]

A company is in business to bring value into the world on some level. It creates an environment that allows for individuals to express their talents, passions, and strengths in a way that will move the organization forward. The profits are a *result* of those efforts. The bigger purpose of the company is the value that it is bringing into the world through its mission and vision.

Many of The Most Amazing Companies focus on stakeholder value—which includes the employees, the customers, *and* the shareholders. When you focus on the people and purpose, the profits will come as a result from those efforts. And many amazing companies have structured some sort of profit sharing. At John Lewis, for example, employees are partners with a stake in the company. "As a Partnership, we are a democracy – open, fair and transparent. Our profits are shared, our Partners have a voice and there is a true sense of pride in belonging to something so unique and highly regarded."[67]

We have heard over and over how frustrated CEOs and MDs of publicly traded companies are because of the shortsightedness of the stock market and the quarterly reporting. It is time to realize that by focusing on the stakeholders, and not purely the stockholders, that the purpose of the company will be fulfilled through a higher productivity which naturally leads to higher profits. There is a bit of a domino effect here, and, in the end, the stockholders *will* be taken care of by higher profits anyway. There is just a slight shift in focus and it can make an enormous difference for a company.

We came across a study[68] that looked at all the companies of the S&P 500 list of companies over a twelve-year period (from 1998 to 2010) and the average return on investment for these companies was 3 percent. Then they analyzed companies on Fortune's Top 100 Best Companies to Work for list. In these companies, the average ROI was 11 percent over the same twelve-year period.[69]

A recent study from the Russell Investment Group reported a significant market increase between FORTUNE Magazine's 100 Best Companies to Work For list versus the S&P 500. If you were to invest in the S&P 500 during 1998-2010, you would gain 3.83 percent return on investment. However, if you had invested in FORTUNE's list, you would gain 11.06 percent in shareholder return. FORTUNE's 100 Best Companies to Work For list is comprised of employers that offer dream workplaces, and are measured on employee satisfaction scores.

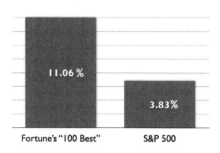

Even the companies listed in Jim Collin's book, *Good to Great*, haven't been performing to the level that many value driven companies have been during the last ten years. Amazing Companies are breaking the models, investing heavily in their people, connecting deeply with their customers, and outperforming more traditionally run companies. They have discovered a new formula that puts the focus on the purpose and the people first.

There is no mistake that companies that invest in their people and the culture create an environment that increases productivity and profits. This is the new business mindset.

In this section, we will take a brief look at some of the progressive thinking that can help increase profits: Marketing, Sales and Innovation, Customer Service, and Efficiency.

1. Marketing, Sales & Innovation

These three areas are very broad and deserve a book a piece at least. There are already hundreds of books that cover these topics much better than we ever could in the scope of this book. However, there are some trends that are changing the way we work and we want to bring that into the framework of our system. Suffice it to say, each topic is very broad and we'll only be touching on a few points.

■ Marketing

Marketing is in the process of evolving. It is about having conversations with customers and because of technology changes and customer sophistication rising, it's changing the way companies need to communicate with their customers in a pretty dramatic way. As Alex Fergusson, Head of Marketing for Virgin Balloon Flights, summed up so well, "We can't control the message anymore. You have to get into the conversation."

No longer is advertising working as well as it used to and there are big disruptive changes facing that branch. What we see happening in many industries is that the middle men are getting cut out of the picture. It means that communicating directly to your customers is becoming easier and much less expensive. But as a company and a brand, you must have strategies that are effective and that means staying on top of how customers *want* to be communicated to.

Essentially, there is so much noise out there and people are so bombarded by messages, it is crucial to first be remarkable—as Seth Godin says—in order to get their attention and then connect on a deeper level to keep it.

We are talking about emotional marketing where you connect to your customers from a value perspective. Because customers are becoming savvy due to the availability of information, it is important to get their attention through a value connection so that they will want to interact with you as a company.

The old school marketing formula has been "problem, agitate, solve". Lisa Manyon, an award-winning author, marketing consultant, and copywriting strategist, offers a new marketing model based on integrity that is much more effective.

1. **Challenge:** Know your ideal clients have challenges. Acknowledge them. Understand them. Don't dwell on them or try to "agitate" or exaggerate the situation.

2. **Solution:** Offer a genuine solution to eliminate or alleviate the challenge. Come from a place of service first. Build relationships with your solution.

3. **Invitation:** Avoid hard sell tactics at all costs. Instead extend a friendly invitation to take the next step and move toward the solution. This is also considered your "call to action". It's extended in a way that builds relationships and treats people as people; not numbers.[70]

Unfortunately for marketers, the buying process is not linear, and, in fact, now buyer behaviors are all over the board. However, there is an interesting step that has been added to the mix from the traditional process of stimulus (such as an ad on TV), to shelf (the point of sale), to experience (taking the product home or using the service). It's called the "zero moment of truth", or ZMOT, and is referring to the step where a consumer is researching a particular brand to get educated and do comparison shopping. It is influencing 84 percent of buying decisions and this is why it is so important to be able to understand as a brand you must be ready to meet the consumer where they are and be proactive with your digital footprint. Google has put together a great website with research to educate marketers on the best ways to reach consumers given this new model.71 You can find out more at www.ZeroMomentofTruth.com.

Zero Moment of Truth

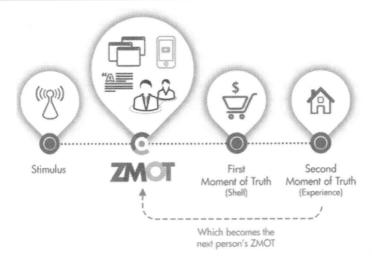

Stimulus   ZMOT   First Moment of Truth (Shelf)   Second Moment of Truth (Experience)

Which becomes the next person's ZMOT

The other aspect of marketing that we see shifting as well is that the communication of the organization both internally and externally much be congruent. That means the marketing and communications need to work closely with human resources so that the organization has a feeling of cohesiveness.

We have already entered a time where conversation is driving the customer relationship. A company must know how, where, when, and, most importantly, why, in order to reach their customers and develop a connection based on values and purpose. This can best be achieved through transparency, integrity, and authenticity in their communications. Lisa Manyon summed it up well in a conversation we had: "The new way of marketing is with truth and integrity that integrates values and comes from a place of service first."

As we mentioned earlier, Cultural Creatives are one of the fastest growing market segments. They are value driven and many of the old business practices simply do not fly with them. They demand authenticity, transparency, values, and a greater purpose from the companies they are consciously choosing to support... or not.

■ Sales

Sales is the lifeblood of the organization. Without sales, the company would cease to exist. Sales is essential, and what we are seeing is that, although the marketing and communications may be shifting, the fundamentals of sales are not. Top sales people are able to connect well with their customers, provide great service, and deliver what they promised. And although technology is changing the way we are interacting and communicating with customers, the relationship between a salesperson and a customer is still strong. People buy from people they like and want to do business with. That is not something that will be changing anytime.

What is changing a bit is that people want to buy from a value driven decision making process. Does this company represent something that I want to spend my hard earned income on? And sales people need to make sure they are including the values and finding that common ground to connect with their customers. When a company has invested the time and effort in the foundational work— the purpose, values, mission, and vision—that is in alignment with how the employees think and feel, and give the unique experience that creates Raving Fans to their customers, then the sales process becomes much more of a matchmaking process.

By connecting to customers from a value perspective, in the long run it actually shortens the purchasing cycle because they already believe in what you are doing. So the key is to connect to your potential customers, give them valuable information over time, and be ready to catch them when they are ready to purchase. It is about building the relationships.

Apple has been an excellent example of emotional branding and creating the desire for new products so that the sales come as a *result* of their previous marketing and communications actions. They are renowned for launching a new product and having people camping out in lines just to purchase them. That is what can happen with emotional branding and creating a strong customer relationship. It will be interesting to follow Apple's journey as the markets change and how they continue without Steve Jobs at the helm.

■ Innovation

Right now we are facing some of the biggest challenges globally. We have issues that are affecting all of humanity and life as we know it. But this also means we are in a time of the greatest opportunities. It is a time for creativity and innovation to solve our current problems.

Plus with the accelerated pace of technology changes, many of the problems we'll have in the next two to five years don't even exist today. That means that students going to college today are going to be learning information that will be obsolete as they enter the work force. We must open our minds to allow for the flexibility and creativity to flow.

This requires a new mindset, an agility and ability to adapt quickly. When the values and purpose are clear on an individual basis, it makes it easier for that person to stay in a place of balance as they face changes, challenges, and problems that they couldn't foresee.

When a company allows for a culture of creativity and innovation, amazing ideas can come forth to take the company forward and gain more clients, give greater service, and continue in fulfilling its purpose.

With so much of what we have already discussed, innovation becomes a result of setting the right culture for the company. We discovered a forward thinking electricity company based in Stock-holm. The energy industry is quite traditional and slow moving when it comes to changes. GodEl (which means good electricity in Swedish) is an electricity company that was founded in 2005 with the mindset of giving back. All of their profits go to chari-ties and good causes. We'll discuss that aspect of them more a bit later. Their biggest challenge in breaking into this market was making it easy for customers to switch electricity compa-nies. After several months struggling, they finally implemented a power of attorney giving them the ability to take care of all the paperwork so that all the customer had to do was sign one paper and they could switch. At the time, this was an innovative and disruptive change that made their business take off. Shortly after, all the other electricity suppliers implemented the same policy.

It was Mark Twain who said, "To succeed in life, you need two things: ignorance and confidence." Entrepreneurs are causing disruptive change with their creative and innovative ideas and starting companies that are here to solve major problems; how-ever, established companies have the systems and resources in place to do the same... as long as they allow innovation and cre-ativity to flourish.

One such company that we talked to based in the Nordics is Proffice, one of the largest staffing companies with upwards of 9,000 employees and consultants. One of their innovative ideas was precisely this: to allow creative ideas from within to be researched and presented as viable business opportunities in what they refer to as opportunity labs. Ideas are presented and then the viable ones are chosen to move forward. They commit to giving the resources to start up new units within the organization—they call this ProLabs, which is essentially a divi-sion for intrapreneurs to grow themselves... and the business.

Many companies have similar initiatives that allow innovation to come from within. This model is a triple win: employees win because they are supported in an entrepreneurial effort, companies win because they create a new business division, and customers win because they have new products or services coming from an established company.

2. Customer Service

Your customers are your lifeline to the business. It is essential that you can give them a unique experience with a WOW factor so that they will continue to come back. In order to take the very best care of them, your customer service needs to be outstanding.

Zappos has really focused in on their customer service department, hiring the right personalities—people who are friendly, outgoing, able to maintain a positive perspective and who are very solution oriented—and they have empowered their customer service department to make sure that the customers are taken care of in the best possible way.

Even entire countries are jumping on the band wagon! Singapore has a national movement called GEMS: Go the Extra Mile for Service. They've been working for years to instill a service mindset on a national level.

Nordstrom's philosophy sums it up well:

Customer service is not a strategy.
Customer service is a way of life.

They believe that you need to "Hire the smile and train the skill." Good advice when it comes to taking care of your customers. When you empower your employees to take ownership, you are giving them the tools to deliver great service and build great relationships with your customers.

Obviously, customer service is very important for maintaining the business. However, we like to show that *every* single person in a company has customers—those are the people they are meant to serve. The marketing and sales forces are the ones who will be attracting and closing the customers. The front line customer service employees are the ones who are taking care of the customers.

But even though someone in accounting, R&D, management, HR, or other support functions may not have as much direct customer contact on a regular basis, they have their own "customers" within the company that they need to deliver great service to. Southwest Airlines has a team dedicated to internal customer care. This small team is responsible for keeping track of the personal life events happening in all of their 46,000 employees! They keep track of birthdays, weddings, births, deaths, personal crises, and send out cards, gifts, support, or whatever is appropriate. When some of their employees were deployed to military service, this team not only sent letters to the soldiers; they sent letters and packages to their families! Not everyone has the resources to allocate for that, but it shows the spirit of caring and internal customer service. This genuine caring is what creates Raving Fans of your employees. Why not encourage everyone to take on a very customer oriented mindset to deliver the best possible service to whomever they might be serving?

The 10 keys to good customer service are:[72]

1. **Create an inviting place for your customers**—whether it is in a physical location like an office or store, online with your website, or by phone.

2. **Give your customers choices**—of products, services, and service channels. Listen closely to deliver what they are looking for and want.

3. **Build the relationship through a deeper value connection**—service your customers through the products and services you offer, but also be clear on your values and what the company stands for.

4. **Hire nice, motivated people**. Getting the right people in the right positions is essential. Understanding your culture and actively working with it makes this process easier as the right people will self select to come work for your company.

5. **Empower employees to take ownership**. The more they feel they can influence and have the power to make a difference, they more they will.

6. **Have compassion and understanding**—consider the customer's point of view in all interactions with them. Be sure to let them know you understand, so that you can move forward to take care of their needs.

7. **Give support and mentoring to your front line employees**. Sustain the people on the front lines through a culture of empowerment and support. This means that the customer service mindset must go deep into the organization.

8. **Celebrate company heroes through recognition and praise.** We can't emphasize this enough. People want to feel valued. Be creative in your recognition strategies and listen to what your employees need. And give praise often!

9. **Bring out the best in others.** Advocate teamwork through internal customer service to deliver the very best. Create a culture where people strive to be the best that they can be.

10. **Commit 100 percent to service on *all* levels**. Having engaged employees is essential to giving great customer service. Allow everyone to define exactly who their customers are and let them start thinking of ways they can over deliver. When you can make this process fun for everyone, it becomes like a game and will bring energy and excitement into the company.

Seth Godin made popular the concept that each person has a tribe of people they are meant to be with and to serve. We believe the world is evolving to take on a more humanistic approach in business, to understand that we are here to make a positive difference in other's lives, and to discover just who those people are.

When you can foster a culture and environment of customer service within your organization on all levels, you are helping your employees to reach their highest potential as they learn to give great service to the people with whom they interact with on a daily basis.

Customer service isn't just for the customer service department or staff. It's for each and every person to embrace and understand exactly who their customers are, and how can they improve that relationship and make sure that they are having a wonderful, unique experience that will turn them into Raving Fans.

We found that there are four keys to delighting your customers from best-selling author of the book, *The Leader Who Had No Title*, by Robin Sharma[73]:

1. **Talk to Your Customers:** A problem is nothing more than an opportunity to engage with the people who keep you in business. This is an opportunity to wow them.

2. **Listen and Say You're Sorry:** Words have power. By taking the responsibility for any sort of complaint and then taking action to resolve the situation as efficiently as possible, this will go a long way with your customers.

3. **Show a Little Humanity:** By connecting to them with understanding and compassion, you are able to take the customer relationship beyond the issue and work to give them what they need.

4. **Go Beyond Expectations:** When you are able to give your customers an experience that exceeds their expectations, they will remember and come back. But, even more so, the more you can exceed their expectations, the higher chance you have of having them become one of your ambassadors out in the world.

We are no longer dealing with just one person, one customer. They have their network that they communicate with whether it's just their family and friends, or all their online connections with Facebook friends and fans, Twitter and Instagram followers, and any sort of online networking groups they are involved in.

As we personally are involved in several mastermind type groups, let me tell you we are sharing both our positive and our negative experiences with products or services we are using. There is no way for a company to actively monitor that other than to understand your customers have an audience and to make sure that you are keeping them happy!

A spokesperson from Ben & Jerry's shared a story about customer service going above and beyond the norm. They invited several customers who had not been 100 percent happy with their ice cream to come to their factory and get a full day tour. It was an experience that one said he felt like being to Willy Wonka's factory with a golden ticket.[74]

In a letter from another customer afterwards, he stated, "The enthusiasm for Ben & Jerry's throughout the day was palpable. It's clear that the joy Ben & Jerry's brings is a direct reflection of the amazingly dedicated and passionate staff that makes up the Ben & Jerry's family." They did this trip because they truly do care what their customers think and take action to improve when there are complaints.[75]

"Business brilliance is pretty simple. Maybe not easy. But pretty simple. And it begins with caring about the people who keep you going." — *Robin Sharma*

Focusing on instilling a customer service mindset in your company on all levels will help to inspire people to be the very best versions of themselves. They will feel proud and accomplished as they improve the lives of others through their interactions. This brings a positive energy into a company that spreads and helps create happy customers and happy employees.

When Does Customer Service Excellence Become 'Legendary'?
By Ron Kauffman

Legendary Service

Many organizations use this phrase to describe and promote their service. But how many have really earned the right to claim customer service excellence?

If you give good service, that's not legendary. If you go out of your way for someone, that's not legendary either. But if you provide service unsurpassed in your field, that can be legendary service. Customer service excellence sets a company apart.

Many years ago I lived in the northeastern United States: cold winters, lots of snow, great skiing. I bought a pair of silk long underpants by mail order from a company called L.L. Bean. The silk was smooth and comfortable, the underpants nice and warm. The product quality spoke to customer service excellence.

(continued)

Then I moved, and moved again, and again. I found myself 20 years later unpacking boxes of clothing in Singapore. There were the old silk underpants.

They were not much use to me now, living near the equator. And even less attractive because they had holes in the knees and were fraying at the ends.

I almost threw them away, then remembered that L.L. Bean features a "lifetime guarantee."

I put the underpants in a plain, brown envelope and inserted a simple handwritten note: "Please replace these."

I didn't have the company's full address. I had not ordered clothing from them for years. On the outside of the envelope I wrote: L.L. Bean, Customer Service, Maine, USA.

At the post office I felt foolish mailing back such a ragged piece of clothing. It didn't seem right to send old underpants all the way around the world by airmail. So for a dollar I sent them the slow way, by sea fully anticipating that customer service excellence had its limits.

Time passed and I forgot all about it, thinking customer service excellence had a time limit. Life quickly filled with new sports, new clothing, and new underpants.

Two months later an envelope arrived from L.L. Bean. Inside was a money order for one dollar. No explanation, just a dollar. I figured they evaluated the old clothing and calculated its leftover value! I laughed and forgot about it. Another month passed and a bigger envelope arrived. Inside was a

(continued)

brand new pair of silk long underpants. Same size and color as the old ones, but brand new!

In time, new catalogs arrived from L.L. Bean and I bought some new clothes. I always feel safe buying from them. I know from experience their "lifetime guarantee" is real and they take customer service excellence seriously.

Months later I was in the United States and called to place a holiday order for some relatives. Chatting with the L.L. Bean telephone representative, I told her the story of returning my old underpants.

"One thing still confuses me," I confessed. "What was the one dollar money order for?"

Laughing, she replied, "Before replacing your underpants, we refunded your postage!"

Twenty-year-old underpants, gladly replaced, including refund of the postage. That's extraordinary. That's truly amazing. *That* is Legendary Service. L.L. Bean understands what customer service excellence is all about.

Key Learning Point For Customer Service Excellence

Using the words "legendary service" is not enough to make it real. You must expand, imagine, innovate - and *take* real legendary action to prove customer service excellence.

Action Steps For Customer Service Excellence

A legend is a story people talk about with admiration and praise, recounting some great deed done in the service of

(continued)

others. What great deed can you do for customers that is admirable, praise-worthy and *truly unsurpassed*? Customer service excellence is a title that's earned, not self-endowed. *Copyright, Ron Kaufman. Used with permission. Ron Kaufman is the world's leading educator and motivator for upgrading customer service and uplifting service culture. He is author of the bestselling "UP! Your Service" books and founder of UP! Your Service. To enjoy more customer service training and service culture articles, visit www.UpYourService.com.*

3. Efficiency

In order to maximize the profits of an organization, you need high productivity and people engagement, great marketing and sales, creativity and innovation, outstanding customer service, and then the processes you have within the company need to be efficient. A company is a system of systems and they need to be efficient to run smoothly. Although there are many continuous improvement tools and methods that can be implemented such as Six Sigma, Kaizen, Lean, all of which have had a major impact on industries and companies, we feel that it's time to go to the next level with this too.

While continuous improvement is definitely something to instill in an organization and everyone should be aware of how they can do their tasks better, it should not become the sole focus. The customer, and the unique experience they have with you, is what should always stay in the forefront of everyone's mind. How you can improve the processes within an organization to lower the costs and increase the productivity can even be detrimental to an organization if they lose touch with the customer and what they want. This has happened with many companies as new emerging technologies bring disruptive innovations to the market that change customer behaviors—it causes the dema-terialization of an industry. An example of this is how technol-ogy has driven the music consumption from records and tapes to CD's, MP3 players, and iPhones, and more recently to Spotify and cloud-based solutions.

Because technological change is increasing so quickly, we need to release a rigid hold to processes and become much more fluid and adaptable while at the same time, keeping a level of high productivity and efficiency. Our technological advances are helping tremendously just by their nature with many tasks and processes but it is also calling for a more discerning ability to be proactive to our customers, our world, and to our own personal space and time.

Technology is taking care of many tasks to help efficiency but it is also creating an overload that affects efficiency. Email is an excellent example of this. When it first started in the 90's it was a novelty to be able to communicate within seconds. It has helped speed decisions up, decrease the need for travel and meetings, and more… but it has now gone overboard in that too many people feel bombarded with messages. It is estimated that we are receiving over 3,000 marketing messages per day through various sources! As one busy HR Director we talked to said, "I get over 350 emails per day! It's not possible to read them all, so I just skim and hope to pick out the right ones that I need to take care of."

When you are leading with your purpose and values, a lot of the "small stuff" gets taken care of. Decisions become much easier to make because they fall within the parameters of the business values, mission, and purpose. By allowing employees to become empowered and responsible for their tasks and their contribu-tion to the organization, rather than trying to micromanage effi-ciency, you will increase both the productivity and the wellbeing of employees.

Here are 11 simple ideas that can help to increase workplace efficiency.

1. **Empower the staff to be on the looking for ways that things can be improved.** Rather than following a rigid system, let the employees take ownership and even give out prizes (that mean something for the employees) for the best suggestions on a monthly basis. By making it a fun process, you'll get more people involved.

2. **Centralize a place for questions or suggestions.** Instead of being interrupted with questions, create an inbox or a forum where people can just submit their questions or ideas. Email can be the best option, or even the old-fashioned suggestion box can do the trick. An open culture tends to create a helpful, supportive environment.

3. **Eliminate unnecessary meetings.** Don't have meetings for the sake of having a meeting just because it's done each week or month. Eliminate all unnecessary meetings. Make sure that the meetings you do have are planned with a specific objective and agenda beforehand. Meetings need to have a strong enough purpose to pull people away from their work.

4. **Praise immediately, specifically, and publicly.** By praising an employee of a job well done quickly and publically, you motivate everyone to want to improve. Be generous with positive feedback. Most supervisors know this but to do it effectively; it must also be done specifically. Tell them exactly what they did that was good. There are some great systems to encourage recognition and praise that can be implemented in a company.

5. **Create a fun environment.** People will work more efficiently when they enjoy their work. It energizes

them and helps them think creatively. When people dislike, or are bored with, their work, they become disengaged. Some employers think that creating a fun environment will slow efficiency but quite the opposite is true. This is especially true among high skilled professionals.

6. **Hire the right people**. Take the time to examine potential employees and explore their values. Learn how to pick and choose the best ones for the job. Involve others in the process to confirm a good value match. Remember that when you can match the personality and values of a person with the culture of the company, it will increase the likelihood that the person will stay longer.

7. **Get organized.** Encourage an organized environment. On a personal level, a cluttered desk or office will make productivity suffer. The same is true for a much larger workplace shared by employees. Supplies should be readily available and easy to get. Help by making the supplies readily available.

8. **Strive to maintain an emply inbox.** Because so many people are overwhelmed with their inboxes, a good goal is to have an empty inbox. With every email (or document) that comes in, you have 3 choices: answer, file, or delete. The goal is to touch each one just once.

9. **Ask employees for workplace productivity ideas**. By asking and listening, it brings a vested interest to improving the organization. Ownership is what makes it work.

10. **Find out what motivates employees**. Allow everyone to share their big dreams and goals in a way so that others can help to support them in reaching them. For any prizes you give away, have employees make a list of things they personally would like to win and then give them something from their list when they do win.

11. **Get key employees to increase their productivity first.**
    The more key people working at a productive level,
    the more buy-in from other employees. Leading by
    example is an effective way to ingrain behaviors in an
    organization.

Having efficient workplace productivity is definitely important
in increasing the bottom line. And this is something that can be
nurtured into the company culture.

■ Wellbeing of Employees

Many of our Amazing Companies are so focused on the people and making sure that they are feeling well, it increases the
productivity and efficiency of the company because people are
happy. Again, we come back to happiness and wellbeing within
the work place.

Our bodies are like very advanced machines. If they are properly taken care of, such as "well-oiled", with the proper nutrition
and rest, as well as being hydrated enough and exercised, they
will continue to perform for a long time. Our average lifespan
has more than doubled in the last century. We are living thirty
years longer than our great grandparents much due to health
and technological advances.

However, stress is the underlying cause of some of the most
deadly diseases and unfortunately, we have created a very
stressful world. It is amazing how we are learning about the
human body's ability to self heal. We can regenerate and
heal because our cells are replacing themselves all the time.
It has been said that it takes anywhere from two to ten years
(depending on how you measure it) to have the trillions of cells
in your body regenerated. Many parts are replaced in a few
short weeks or months.

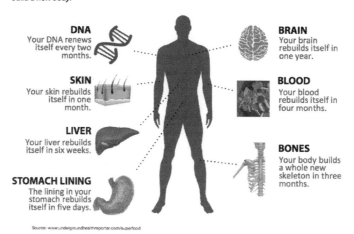

How your Body rebuilds itself in less than 365 days

FACT: *Your entire body totally rebuilds itself in less than two years – and 98% in less than 365 days. Every cell in your body eventually dies and is replaced by new cells. Every day is a new opportunity to build a new body.*

DNA
Your DNA renews itself every two months.

SKIN
Your skin rebuilds itself in one month.

LIVER
Your liver rebuilds itself in six weeks.

STOMACH LINING
The lining in your stomach rebuilds itself in five days.

BRAIN
Your brain rebuilds itself in one year.

BLOOD
Your blood rebuilds itself in four months.

BONES
Your body builds a whole new skeleton in three months.

Source: www.undergroundhealthreporter.com/superfood

What this means is that we can help the people in our companies reach their full potential by encouraging smart choices for their wellbeing. This is why so many companies are investing in offering healthy, nutritious meals. Google has gourmet meals 24 hours a day. DHL has hired some of the best chefs to prepare the meals in their corporate restaurants. Companies have invested in building gyms and offering exercises classes on site. And others, such as John Lewis and Electrawinds, are combining people's passions and hobbies and creating groups of employees that are participating in their favorite sports together, such as running, biking, surfing, skiing, and many others.

Some companies are even bringing meditation and mindfulness into the work place. Mindfulness Gruppen, a Stockholm based consultancy specializing in teaching mindfulness, has seen an increase in business as leaders understand that they just feel better, are calmer, and have stronger relationships by bringing mindfulness into their lives and workplace. And MindValley, a company that has a mission to bring meditation to the world and has grown significantly over the last few years showing that there is an interest and a demand for this learning, has a group meditation they lead as a part of their weekly company meeting.

An interesting side note we recently came across regarding mediation...scientists have measured that the alpha state brain waves, which is the state of deep relaxation often reached through meditation, are 7.83 Hz. The planet also has an electromagnetic frequency which measures in at the exact same level of 7.83 Hz. There is no coincidence in this and it is known as Schumann Resonance. The Institute of Heartmath that has been scientifically studying the heart for over twenty years now refers to this as global coherence. More and more science is proving the importance of connection, not only between people but also with all living forms including our planet.

In these crazy busy days, it sometimes means slowing down to increase efficiency and productivity. This is because slowing down can allow us to tap into our creative resources. We are shifting from a place where *having* was the most important aspect to where *being* has taken the lead. We want to *be* happy and productive. We want to be connected to that higher purpose that gives our lives meaning. We want to reach our highest potential. Our work gives us the biggest chance for this.

Companies have the greatest opportunity to give employees the ability to express their greatest potential. The discussion about work-life balance is important because we are starting to see each individual as a whole and finding ways to support employees wellbeing is good business sense because it will increase loyalty, enthusiasm, and engagement in the company which will return in a better customer relationships, increased productivity and the result from that tends to be higher profits.

■ Measuring Metrics

As we have discussed, there is tremendous pressure with listed companies and their quarterly reporting. The retail industry is known for their low wages and the "burn and churn" mentality in how they treat employees. Just compare the reputations of Costco with Wal-Mart in the US. These two giants have taken a very different approach in the values of building the businesses and how they treat employees. Costco pays significantly more to their employees and therefore have a more stable, loyal, happy workforce. "Instead of minimizing wages, we know it's a lot more profitable in the long term to minimize employee turnover and maximize employee productivity, commitment, and loyalty," said Craig Jelinek, Costco's chief executive.[76]

Whereas Wal-Mart seems to be continually in the news with protests and unhappy employees barely making ends meet. They are facing tremendous pressure as their workers unite to demand better working conditions. With over two million employees, even though they may be ranked high at number three on the Fortune's 500 list, there is a huge value gap and they are going to have to make significant strides in order to stay in the new game of doing business. Instead of creating Raving Fans, they are creating Raving Protesters!

We believe it is time to seriously re-evaluate what we are measuring and counting towards success. This is why we love GameChangers 500. Andrew Hewitt, the founder of this organization, is measuring and informing the market of companies that are evaluated for innovation, employee wellbeing, and environmental impact. Within each category, there are three badges that companies can earn. Inspired by wanting to find a more tangible way of rating companies rather than just the revenues and profits such as the Fortune 500 list Andrew and GameChangers 500 are leading us into new ways of looking at the world.

We recently heard of a new way of measuring a company using "Positive Measurable Impact Metrics" AKA PMI Metrics. These are humanized metrics to be used in combination with traditional cold metrics and analysis. Caleb Jennings is a co-founder of Young and Raw, a progressive online health and wellness website that is bringing an awareness that food is the foundation of our lives and how we feel. He told us measuring PMIs have changed the way they do everything. In his own words:

> *"It will be different for every company, and core values are the guiding light for defining which PMI metrics are most important and take priority. For us, we track such metrics as how much weight our customers lose, how much lean muscle they gain if working out, how many chronic disorders are healed, reversed etc., how many cases of Diabetes are healed reversed or able to be managed with little to no medication, how many prescriptions our customers get rid of as a result of following our cleanses and recommendations, how many families and children are integrating healthier real food and healthy habits in their lifestyle inevitably pushing the junk "phoods" out over time and other metrics along those lines... It's quite a work in progress, although this system has completely changed the way we do just about everything, and it keeps us super stoked, jacked on life, and passionately in love with what we do."*

As we move into our final section of our book, Positive Impact, we can start to consider exactly what the most important factors are that companies can contribute with through their efforts in making the world a better place for everyone.

13

Positive Impact

The last segment of our core element model is positive impact. Over and over, The Most Amazing Companies are clear on their bigger purpose and have a fully engaged workforce which is highly productive and passionate about their work. They are profitable and because of all these elements working together, they are able to have a positive impact on some level in the world.

Contribution is a core trait with Amazing Companies. They believe in giving back and because it's such an integral part of their culture, it gives their employees a feeling of doing something that matters. A big shift that has happened in the last few years is that people are becoming much more conscious about humanity and have a deep desire to do something good. They want to make a difference.

Best-selling author and high performance business mentor, Brendon Burchard, always asks three questions:

- Did I live?
- Did I love?
- Did I matter?

This is a reflection of the general population who are asking these questions more and more. We see that companies offer the ideal environment for everyone to fulfill their higher purpose and feel like they matter—if they work actively to create this opportunity for their employees. Multiple studies and surveys indicate that employees are seeking meaningful work much more so than pay increases or benefits.

Whether the positive impact is on a small or large scale is not so important. What matters is that there is a value based contribution to either the local communities, to the planet, and to the betterment of humanity on some level. For example, Costco and Electrawinds have extensive meetings with the local communities before they begin to build to make sure that they can address the local concerns. They are genuinely connecting to their customers in a way that makes them feel heard and cared for, which has a positive ripple effect.

Customers also resonate more with the bigger purpose and what a company is doing to make the world a better place. No longer are there isolated and private markets. With the shift in technology that is only going to be increasing, customers want to know how responsible a company is. Corporate social responsibility (CSR) has gained traction in many corporations and The Most Amazing Companies have evolved to the next level where their contribution or positive impact is an important part of their business model...and their business mindset.

In this final section, we will discuss Raving Fans, Maximizing Potential with employees, and lastly the Contribution Code—an important key to Amazing Companies and engagement.

1. Raving Fans

This is really one of the most important elements of creating an Amazing Company. We define Raving Fans as people who love what you do so much, that they keep coming back for more and telling all their friends about it. These can and should be all your customers, all your partners (which includes suppliers, vendors, strategic alliances, affiliates, etc), and, of course, all of the employees.

We therefore expand the demographic model to include the customers at the very top because without them, the company would not exist, and the partners who should be brought into the company as an extension of what you do. We call this the shift model.

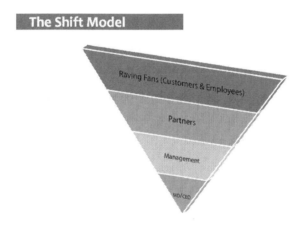

The Shift Model

Raving Fans (Customers & Employees)

Partners

Management

MD/CEO

There are functions within an organization that may feel they are removed from customer contact; however, we see this differently. It doesn't matter whether the customers are external or internal.

Each function in a company serves a certain audience and people must understand that they are there to help others out and improve their lives in some way. Each department must consider who it is they are there to serve in the bigger scope of delivery for the organization and its mission.

While we refer to customers more from the external end user, all of these concepts to turn the people you interact with into Raving Fans apply at all levels. The bottom line is that *everyone* you interact with has the potential to be transformed into a Raving Fan!

- **Customers**—have a unique experience and receive out-standing customer service

Customers are kings. They are the reason a business will even exist. Without customers, you have no business and therefore no reason for being. Taking care of your customers is essential. But we're not talking about satisfied customers. Who wants just satisfied customers? That means they think their experience was "okay". Becoming an Amazing Company is all about getting Raving Fans: customers so happy with you that they want more and more. The repeat business is a no brainer because they absolutely love what you do—and they rave about it to their friends. Which brings in even more customers... and up the upward spiral of growth and profitability you go!

- **Employees** –create an environment where employees love what they are doing

You also want your employees to be your Raving Fans—for a number of reasons. If they love what the company is doing and represents, they will be passionate about their contribution to the mission. If the people in their social circles see how happy they are, it will help the company attract the best talent. Imagine having a waiting list of the best talent out in the world that would love to come work for your company. It's a dream situation for any HR Director! Also, your employees will be more productive when they love what they are doing which results in lower turn-over, lower sick leave, a greater sense of wellbeing which all lead to direct bottom line profitability.

- **Partners**—treat your partners well and as a significant part of your business

When you form such strong alliances with your partners, and you both become an integral part of each other's business, you lift each other as you grow. Having your partners as Raving Fans will not only increase your business, it will naturally increase theirs as well. Collaboration is a new way of sharing the abundance that is available... all it requires is a new mindset and a new perspective of looking at business.

Raving Fans experience the WOW factor and want more. The value they are expecting far exceeds what they thought it should be. During Oprah's twenty fifth and last season of her talk show, Oprah and her team wanted to give a once-in-a-lifetime experience for the ultimate viewers (AKA Raving Fans). They surprised three hundred audience members with an all-expense paid trip to Australia! Now that's a WOW factor that speaks volumes.

Not to get discouraged, because there is only one Oprah on this planet, it is possible to create your own Raving Fans easily. It is a matter of evaluating all of your systems and all of your customer touch points so that you are able to give them the maximum experience at all times. Raving Fans become an extension of your business as they do the word of mouth marketing for you. They are your customer evangelists, your biggest supporters, and they are the result, the gift if you like, to all the work you have done to create an amazing experience for them.

John Lewis states: "We build relationships with our customers, suppliers and each other based on honesty, respect and encouragement."[77] Amazing companies have a high awareness of the importance of their relationships with everyone they come in contact with and they are actively nurturing those relationships to create their Raving Fans.

The Evoloshen Program and System is a step-by-step guide to building the foundation and the entire house to create your Raving Fans.

•Raving Fans! — are passionate about the experience, they are WOW'd and continue to buy all your products/service, tell everyone about it

•Happy Clients —they are happy and are repeat customers, have a more personal relationship, but they don't tell anyone about the experience

•Satisfied Customers —they are ok, might or might not be repeat customers

The Evoloshen Customer Scale

•Dissatisfied Customers – bought once and might give you a second chance—or not

•Disgruntled Purchasers – bought once but won't ever be back and they let you know it

•PR Disaster – had such a negative experience they've created a media & PR nightmare for your company

- Where are the majority of your customers?
- How do you know where your customers (or non-customers) really are?
- What will it take to get them to the top of this scale?

2. Maximizing Potential

In an ever increasing stressful world, resilience is a necessity not only to survival but to knowing how to thrive. The best way to instill this is to allow individuals to optimize their own potential through personal growth. An employee with a balanced life is by far a more productive person who can contribute significantly.

Work-life resilience must be boosted to stay competitive. Fostering a resilient workplace and workers is a necessary component of doing business in an uncertain marketplace. "A person who is resilient has the ability to absorb a great deal of complexity and stress, and still function with grace," says Jennifer Sertl of management strategy company Agility3R.[78] Bouncing back from failure is crucial for productivity, she explains, adding that resilience allows workers to take in a great deal of information and expand their creativity.

- Work-life balance vs. work-life integration

These days it is almost impossible to be unplugged. Finding balance is becoming more and more challenging. But if we change our focus to finding a way to integrate these two parts of our lives, it becomes easier. Part of this is by working on what a person is truly passionate about. Then their work gives them energy—a positive charge—that will flow into other areas of their lives as well.

> "Intellectual growth should commence at birth and cease only at death." — Albert Einstein

■ Allow people to develop as a whole person

Investing in your employees is an investment in the company. Because if each person is growing on a personal level, not just on a professional one, they will have a better outlook on their own lives, a higher sense of wellbeing, and more balance in their lives. Personal development allows each individual to pursue their passions, to find their own higher purpose, and to integrate that into their lives. It is acknowledging the whole person and not only the skills or talents that they bring to the company. This is a humanistic approach and it will pay big dividends over time.

> Almost two decades later, I can still remember some of the personal development programs that my employer, Management Recruiters International invested in my growth. It has had a lasting effect and, in truth, it began my passion for personal development and learning. I will always be grateful for the time and training that my manager invested in me and, although I ended up taking another path, they received a huge value in developing not only myself, but in building a new division, which to this day is one of their largest profit centers. They understood the power of investing in your people.
>
> — Karin Volo

■ Focus on Strengths

Everyone has certain strengths that drive them forward in life. Identifying your strengths, and focusing on them, helps you to get into the flow of life so that things can start happening more easily for you in all areas of your life.

Qualities of Strengths:

- You're better at it and people notice
- You enjoy doing it—it's fun for you!
- You feel alive and energized when doing it
- You continually improve your performance at it
- You experience a state of flow while doing it—you easily lose all track of time

---

Strength = Talents + Experiences + Education + Skills

To identify your true strengths, you'll need to figure out what your talents are, how your experience has made your talents stronger, and what skills you've picked up along the way.

If everyone within the company focused on their strengths, imagine the productivity and results that would happen! Employee engagement would skyrocket, progress would happen on warp speed compared to before, and profits would soar. It is like taking a team of thoroughbred horses and instead of having them work a farm, they are allowed to race as they were born to do. This is a way to supercharge your company from the inside and transform it easily to an Amazing Company very quickly.

■ Enhance the quality of life

Optimizing potential enables us to have a higher quality of life because we are learning, growing, and developing as a person. Life is change, change is constant, growth is optional. Investing time and effort into bettering yourself in some way gives you more energy, new perspectives, and helps you to find new ways to contribute. It puts you in balance with your life and how you want to live it. It is uplifting, inspiring, and expansive, which will overflow into all areas of your life: career, family, relationships, health, etc.

As we have seen already, an employee's wellbeing is instrumental to the success of a company. This applies to their emotional, mental, spiritual, and physical wellbeing. Investing in personal development tends to help the emotional, mental, and spiritual aspects.

The physical aspects are also important. Companies that offer benefits such as health club memberships, or have a gym on site, make it easier for the employees to take the time to exercise. Companies can offer healthy meals on site and even classes on nutrition. As we mentioned earlier, promoting a healthy lifestyle will increase awareness of wellbeing, decrease long term health issues and decrease absenteeism and sick leave. Taking into account the person as a whole shows that the company cares.

■ Contribute to the realization of dreams and aspirations

Most people have dreams or aspirations they would love to achieve. Maximizing potential allows a person to discover these, build on them, and make them happen. If a company or manager can support their employees in pursing these dreams, it increases creativity and loyalty in that person. If those dreams and aspirations can be met within the company you will have a dedicated, productive employee who is fully engaged, happier, and more productive. Creating an environment where people can not only grow but thrive and flourish will make the company more successful.

If it had to be boiled down to three questions that were vital to know about your employees and coworkers, these would tap into their dreams and goals:

- What do I want to experience in my life?
- How do I want to grow?
- How do I want to contribute to the planet?

MindValley gets each employee to write down their goals and dreams following these simple yet profound questions. Then they post the answers on a board that everyone can look at. It shows very openly what motivates and drives each person and connects them on a deeper level. It's a great example of how you can combine personal growth with a Thriving Culture and collaboration.

Another innovative idea that MindValley has implemented in their company is a forty five hour-work week with five of those hours to invest in personal growth. Their employees can choose how and when to use those hours. Since MindValley is a personal development training company, this fits in quite well with their values and mindset. They understand the benefits of investing in their employees because they become more passionate, engaged, and well balanced making them more productive, committed, and happier. It becomes a win-win situation for everyone.

TOMS is also giving their employees opportunities for great life experiences. Every year they take some of the employees on the giving trips when they are delivering the shoes to the children in need. These trips have a deep and profound impact on everyone who goes. It brings tears of joy to most people because they are so moved by the entire experience. What a wonderful way to create more loyalty and desire to be productive for their employees.

There are many creative ways that a company can invest in personal growth, and each organization must find what will work for their culture and values.

3. Contribution Code

There is a big shift happening in how we are looking at the world.

■ Making a difference in the world

If we look at Abraham Maslow's hierarchy of needs: the basic needs, such as food and shelter, must be met first, then security and relationships. Once those have been met, we move into self-esteem needs and then, finally, self actualization where people want to feel a part of something bigger.

Maslow's Triangle

Morality, creativity, spontaneity, problem solving, lack of prejudice, acceptance of facts

Self-actualization

Self-esteem, confidence, achievement, respect of others, respect by others

Esteem

Friendship, family, sexual intimacy

Love/belonging

Security of: body, employment, resources, morality, the family, health, property

Safety

Breathing, food, water, sex, sleep, homeostasis, excretion

Physiological

Anthony Robbins, a world-renown personal development and high potential expert, says there are two primary needs humans have:

1. Spiritual growth and
2. Contributing to the world in some way

In the developed countries, most of our basic needs are being met. Because our standard of living is so much higher now than what it was a century ago, with all of our technological advances, people are feeling discontent and frustrated because they don't need more things in their lives—they need meaning and purpose. Contribution is a way to achieve that.

There is a shift happening in that people are realizing we are all connected on some level.

Here is a true story that exemplifies how we are truly connected.

Wild Elephants Mourn the Death of The "Elephant Whisperer"

Author and legendary conservationist Lawrence Anthony died on March 2, 2012. His family tells of a solemn procession of elephants that defies human explanation.

Lawrence had saved herds of elephants by living with them and gaining their trust after they had been abused and mishandled by others for years. On March 4, two herds had travelled miles from the bush to his home, stayed outside for two days, and then disappeared back into the wild after those two days of mourning.

How is it possible that they had even known he had passed away? Elephants are known for their grieving process and will break out of their habits to mourn. What else could possibly explain such behavior, other than we are all connected on some level?

The Y Generation wants to see a bigger purpose—they want to know how what they are doing makes a difference. They are entering the workforce now and bringing a totally different mind-set and expectation about what work is and they are not willing to sacrifice their values and ideals for anything less than their standard. It is driving change and shaking up the way we have been taught to view the world.

■ Allowing employees to contribute keeps them engaged

Engaged employees—people who feel they enjoy their jobs, who are happy, and who feel they are contributing to something meaningful—are naturally going to be more productive and creative. Again, we come back to the integrated needs of humans to feel they are a part of something bigger. We need meaning in our lives otherwise we feel empty, we can become depressed, and we lose our motivation.

Employees need to understand the bigger picture so that they understand their work is vital to the success of the company, and that they are not just a cog in the machine. This is why it is vital that each individual understands that by doing their very best, by focusing on their expertise, and by continually improving their strengths, they are able to be a part of this shift. They are able to contribute in their own unique and individual ways that make a difference to both the company but more importantly to themselves.

■ The shift from competition to contributism

We are changing from the competition model of business where money is the primary reason for existence to the contributism model of business where our purpose is greater and the profits will naturally grow when we are doing things right.

When your "why" is big enough, you won't have competition because everyone will want you to succeed. Plus you have evolved in your mindset to realize that no matter what, you, your company, and your work are unique. The experience you offer is something that can only come from you, and you realize that the customers or clients you have are the ones you want to have. You do not want to have any and every customer available—you want the ones that are your Raving Fans and that love what you bring to the world.

This shift in mindset will take your company from a commodity model, where features and prices are the driving indicators, to a transformative model where the experience and service is so unique the only place to get it is with you—thus eliminating all concerns about competition. You create your own game!

Your job is to find them and attract them through your marketing and communication and the message you have to share with them.

GodEl, the Swedish electric company, was founded by entrepreneur Stefan Krook, with the sole purpose of giving back. Stefan had early success with another company but then went through a time of major soul searching. He wanted to make sure that what he did contributed back; that it contributed to the world in a meaningful way. The idea of creating a company that gave 100 percent of its profits to worthy causes took hold of his mind. It turned out that the opportunity presented itself to do this with electricity. Since they were founded in 2005, and then up until 2012, they have contributed over $3 million dollars to various charities. The business model clearly works and they have plenty of Raving Fans, both with employees and customers, who will attest to what they are doing.

PUMA is another model company that is lifting their purpose to much higher levels. Because they have such a strong global influence in the sporting world, their impact goes far. They are actively working with environmental conditions, sustainable products to cultivate a safety and they even have an initiative to promote peace. They have understood that it is time to move on from the competitive models of the industrial age towards more collaboration... and joy.

PUMA for Peace

"Herzogenaurach September 22nd, 2009

It was a historic game against an unusual backdrop: Under the leadership of the two chief executives Herbert Hainer (midfielder) and Jochen Zeitz (goalkeeper), employees of both adidas and PUMA played football together and against each other on Monday, Global Peace Day, in Herzogenaurach. With the support of 700 employees of both groups, the "Black" team of the two CEOs beat the "White" team 7:5 in a fascinating game. In support of the peace initiative PEACE ONE DAY the two sportswear companies sent a fun and unique signal of amicable cooperation.

Both teams, which were made up of 40 employees of both competitors as well as a few local journalists, demonstrated their support for PEACE ONE DAY on the premises of the adidas headquarters and proved that sport can help overcome boundaries and promote a peaceful cohabitation.

"Our joint football match in support of PEACE ONE DAY and Global Peace Day was a unique experience for the participating players and our employees. It showed that everyone – and companies as well – can make their contribution to peace," said the two Chief Executives Jochen Zeitz and Herbert Hainer. "The symbolic handshake of adidas and PUMA helped to raise awareness for Global Peace Day and the necessity for non-violence and ceasefire."

(continued)

The companies adidas and PUMA were founded by the brothers Rudolf and Adi Dassler in the 1940s. Until they separated and went their own ways, they both owned a factory called "Gebrüder Dassler Sportschuhfabrik" where they together manufactured sports shoes – quite successfully as the world records of Jesse Owens proved. In the last decades, adidas and PUMA became worldwide leading brands. Both companies are still based in Herzogenaurach, Germany." *PUMA Press Release September 22, 2009*

These two global companies had been in fierce rivalry for years. By taking the initiative to model peace themselves, this has become an integral part of PUMA's mission—to bring more peace into the world. They have sponsored peace matches in 94 countries and a series of films for peace. This is a company that is not only wearing their shoes but they are walking their talk!

The Difference Between Philanthropy and Contribution

Companies will often have a philanthropic arm to their business and that is wonderful. However, giving money to a cause is a big difference to contributing in our viewpoint. When you have contribution as a part of your business strategy from the beginning, it becomes a part of your value system. It is not an afterthought or something you do when you've made your billions.

It is integrated into the way you are growing your business, the way you even conduct business and that is a significant mindset shift. Amazing Companies have contribution as a part of their DNA—they cannot exist without that element or they wouldn't be where they are today. This value driven mindset determines *how* you do business and filters into every action and every decision that is moving the company forward. It is a key strategy to get your employees engaged. "The best form of corporate social responsibility is not making monetary donations to charities, but the dedicated involvement of everyone in a company in meaningful pursuits that transcend the bottom line."[80] Richard Branson, in his book *Screw Business As Usual*, calls this Capitalism 24902 (representing the circumference in miles around the globe). We call it Contributism.

TOMS Shoes established their business using the One-For-One model. For each product sold, another product is given to another in need. After having such success with shoes (giving a pair of shoes to a child in need thereby preventing possible disease), they have expanded now into sunglasses, where they are giving sight to someone in need through eye glasses or eye surgery. This philosophy automatically lifts the customers out of a simple purchase transaction and into a higher cause action. As founder Blake Mycoskie says, "Giving is what fuels us. Giving is our future."[81]

There is a belief that by giving you will receive. Now this is *not* to be interpreted in that you give away your product without receiving compensation. But you do give a high quality sample so that potential customers can decide if this is something for them or not. Just go to any mall and watch them giving away sample tastes of cookies or muffins. The chances of purchasing increase tenfold.

There is an interesting trend occurring in response to customer desires to know which companies are really committed to making a positive impact. A new business corporation structure is emerging called a Benefit Corporation or B Corp. Benefit corporations are exactly the same as traditional corporations except for three little things that make them progressive, leading companies.

Benefit Corporations are required to have the following:

1. *Purpose*: have a corporate purpose to create a material positive impact on society and the environment.
2. *Accountability*: expand fiduciary duty to require consideration of the interests of workers, community and the environment.

3. *Transparency*: publicly report annually on overall social and environmental performance against a comprehensive, credible, independent, and transparent third party standard.

Many companies are proactively taking measures to account for their impact in the world by registering as a B Corp (http://bcorporation.net/) According to Wikipedia, "Triple bottom line (abbreviated as TBL or 3BL, and also known as people, planet, profit or the three pillars) captures an expanded spectrum of values and criteria for measuring organizational (and societal) success: economic, ecological, and social." Benefit corporation legislation not only gives businesses the freedom and legal protection to pursue the triple bottom line but it gives individual citizens something positive for which to advocate.

Contribution takes it up to the next level where you become emotionally involved with the transaction because you believe in the purpose and reason behind the product or service.

Another great resource in response to the market is Game Changers500. Andrew Hewitt, a passionate young man wanting to make a positive difference in the world, saw how so many of his friends ended up miserable in their corporate jobs just a few short years after graduating from college. His journey took him to ask why don't we measure companies on things that make a positive impact? Much like the Fortune 500 list that compiles a yearly list of the top 500 companies based on revenues, GameChangers500 is rating companies on employee wellbeing, innovativeness, and environmental impact.

Albert Einstein said, *"Many of the things you can count, don't count. Many of the things you can't count, really count."* We are seeing that our views of the world are shifting—we want to start counting the things we have not counted before—how we feel, how we impact others, and how we are contributing to make the world a better place for everyone.

PUMA, in collaboration with PwC, has created an environmental P&L. They have calculated a monetary value on the natural resources they are using in their entire supply chain, including land use, air pollution, clean water, etc. If every company was proactive to calculate this, they could be making decisions based on a holistic perspective of the entire ecosystem.

Virgin Unite is the giving arm of the Virgin brand. It started as an initiative from the employees who said they have had such a great track record for starting up businesses that make a difference, so why didn't they use those skills to give back in a significant way—and violá, Virgin Unite was born. Richard Branson covers 100 percent of the operational costs so that all funds that are donated or raised go directly to the programs. With just one of their many projects, Virgin Unite has started two Branson Centers for Entrepreneurship, one in South Africa and the other in the Caribbean, which help to mentor and train entrepreneurs to start up companies and create jobs. They see entrepreneurship as a way to lift a country out of poverty by becoming self sustaining and creating jobs and, therefore, give the support to become successful. Also, 100 percent of Richard's book sales for *Screw Business As Usual* and his speaking fees go directly to Virgin Unite. Jean Oelwang is the CEO and has done an incredible job building a dynamic team that supports a number of progressive initiatives in addition to the Centers for Entrepreneurship, all of which are making a positive impact in local communities and in the world.

Virgin Media in the UK took this inspiration and started Virgin Media Pioneers, a networking and support platform for young entrepreneurs where they can receive mentoring, inspiration, share best practices, and take those steps to start businesses and make a positive difference. This division has even had a major positive influence in the Parliament. They rallied government officials to offer business loans to young entrepreneurs in addition to their student loan program. Their thoughts were "Why should only studying be supported when entrepreneurs are just as important?" Now there is a part of the budget that dedicates over £100 million for new startup companies in the UK.

Most recently, Virgin Unite has been involved in incubating The B Team. Founded by Richard Branson and former PUMA CEO Jochen Zeitz, this new organization is bringing together leaders of major businesses to come up with a Plan B on how to do business. We are so excited to see this initiative as more people join this mission to evolve the way we do business in the world so that it supports the people, the planet, and profits for the benefit of all.

Ben & Jerry's started their foundation when they had their public offering in 1985. Their focus has been to fund grassroots efforts that otherwise might not get funding. What is interesting with their foundation is that they have an employee matching program so when employees donate, the company matches their donation up to $2,000. The foundation's decisions are also made from employee groups, empowering the company from within. They are a leading example of values, contribution, and empowerment.

IKEA also has a foundation that incorporates doing good by focusing on children living in poverty in developing countries by partnering and giving grants to organizations with large infrastructures to make a positive difference. Their employees are able to be selected to go on iWitness Trips so they can learn about the impact of these programs first hand to share with their coworkers and customers, which increases engagement and impact.

All these companies have inspired us to also give back. For every book purchase, we are donating a book to young entrepreneurs and students. The more we can spread this new way of doing business, the greater impact we can have towards working together collectively to make our planet a sustainable and beautiful place to be. Even with our company, Evoloshen, we are giving 50 percent of our profits to support causes we believe in. Giving is how we can truly make a difference.

Contribution also comes in the form of letting employees donate their time towards a cause. We found many examples of this such as Patagonia that offers an Environmental Internship Program giving employees up to eight weeks of paid leave to volunteer for an environmental organization. HCL Technologies in the Nordics, lead by Liselotte Hägertz Engstam, initiated a program with the local schools to teach technical skills which also allowed many of the expat employees to get a better understanding of the cultural nuances in the Nordics. Another Nordic company has had this in their DNA for over fifteen years. Skandia is a Swedish company that started "Ideas for Life" back in the late nineties where employees could volunteer some of their work time towards supporting different initiatives. All of these efforts create a deeper sense of meaning and connection in an employee's life which increases loyalty and retention for the company.

Contribution is playing a major role in the mindset shift of business. And businesses are positioned to make a huge difference in the world. With so many changes happening and old systems falling apart, the corporations and entrepreneurs of the world are perfectly positioned to bridge the shift by creatively solving the problems we are facing on our planet. There is no better time, with huge opportunities abounding, to not only make a significant difference in the world but to capitalize on the solutions.

14

The Shift Formula and TMAC Blueprint

The Shift Formula

The Shift Formula is how you can take an average or even good company and turn it into an Amazing Company. By working on all the elements described here, and engaging the entire organization to implement, improve, create an amazing culture, and exceed everyone's expectations, you will work together in a collaborative way to create not only an Amazing Company but also amazing customers, an amazing workplace, and a much bigger sense of purpose.

Just as a pebble that is dropped into water will create a ripple effect out—doing the internal work within an organization will have positive ripples throughout each employee, each customer, and anyone who comes in contact with the company. When the purpose is clearly defined and the values aligned, a higher level of productivity will result. And all this will naturally lead to higher profits.

When the bigger purpose is defined through a clear vision and mission and the values are aligned in a way that everyone can live and work by them, it begins to create an environment in which everyone can thrive. Getting everyone to understand how they contribute to the organization and they begin to feel valued for what they do will increase retention, which has a direct impact on the bottom line.

We should note that with changes, there will be a certain attrition rate; however, the people who leave because they are uncomfortable with where the company is going are those who will only hold you back from your Amazing Company Quest. By sharing this common quest, the majority of people will embrace the new mindset and see the benefits for both themselves and the company.

One indicator of the times that have changed is an example of a magazine that started in 2010 called *Good News Magazine*. The founder, Daniel Mendoza, was told by many that this idea was never going to work. All the traditional magazines said there was no way it would be successful, they had done their market research. With a shoestring budget *Good News Magazine* was started and has now grown into one of the most popular magazines in the Nordics and growing rapidly. People *do* want to have good news and feel happier.

We are in the midst of a paradigm shift. Companies need to understand how people in general are changing their views. We are seeing the signs much more so in the consumer market but it is not far behind to reach the B2B market either. Therefore, companies can be proactive rather than reactive, and take steps to reach their full potential by focusing on their employees and their customers by creating an experienced based model that connects and inspires others.

By taking steps to work through this shift formula, the ultimate outcome for each person leads to happiness and wellbeing, which in turn, leads to higher productivity and profits for the organization. In the end, shareholder value increases anyway because the company has transformed itself to an Amazing Company and the employees and customers have become Raving Fans. It is a triple win!

The Value of Happiness and Wellbeing

Everyone ultimately is after the same thing in life: being happy. The paths we take are all different and vary with as many people we have on the planet but the ultimate desire is the same. There are four parts to happiness:

- Perceived control
- Perceived progress
- Connectedness
- Vision/meaning

People want to feel in control of their lives, they need to see positive progress, there needs to be a level of connectedness in their relationships with others, and there must be a clear vision and purpose or meaning in doing what they do. When those elements are present, the level of contentment and happiness increase dramatically.

Vishen Lakhiani, founder of MindValley, says that happiness is the new productivity. We believe he's 100% correct. A company that cares about its employees and helps to create an incredible environment where they can grow and flourish, whose focus is on creating Raving Fans in all the people who interact with the company, who is clear on its Bigger Purpose and is contributing to the world to make it a better place, is bound to have amazing results.

They say you can't buy happiness...but in fact you can, if it's done the right way. Michael Norton, an associate professor at Harvard Business School, gave a TED TALK called "How To Buy Happiness".[82] His research showed that when you spend money on others, you become happier. Across the globe in a survey by Gallup, it showed that people became happier when they spent money on others. When they did this experiment within companies, the ROI was significant. When employees were given €15 to spend on personal incentives, the ROI was only €4.50 so it showed money was actually lost. However, when the same €15 was spent on pro-social incentives, the ROI was an astounding €78!

Shawn Achor, author of *The Happiness Advantage—Linking Positive Brains to Productivity,* explains that when dopamine floods your system when you are positive, it has two functions:

- it makes you happier
- it turns on all the learning centers in your brain allowing you to adapt to the world in a different way

Happiness and wellbeing clearly are essential to the future of business. We are in a Shift of mindset and our old ways of doing business simply are not sustainable. In order to move into the new paradigm, we must evolve as a species, but also as a culture. Our business world must also evolve to the next level. It must adapt quickly to not only survive but also to thrive.

We are at a point in time where we have some of the largest global challenges we've ever faced: economic meltdown, changing weather patterns causing extreme weather shifts, an unsustainable dependency on fossil resources that are damaging the environment, extinction of multiple species upsetting the natural food chain, rampant disease, stress levels and depression at all time highs... the list goes on and on. But we are also at the point of greatest opportunity. Never before have we had such an incredible chance to make a difference not only in our communities but on a global scale.

Technology has connected our world in a way that transcends borders. Our business world today is much like the tribal nations of long ago but with much better communication. By working in a collaborative way to make a positive impact on the world, businesses can rapidly make the shift to improve our current state. With companies bringing a higher standard of shared values, products, and services that can solve our current day issues, they are relevant and can capitalize on the shift our planet is experiencing.

The Evoloshen System helps companies to integrate all the elements that lead to highly productive employees, that create Raving Fans, and that raises the company to reach new levels of collaboration, creativity, connection, celebration, and contribution which all lead to higher profitability and greater impact.

Happiness, or joy, is the key ingredient to creating an amazing life, an Amazing Company, and an amazing world. We were not put on this planet to dread one third of our lives—is that really progress for humanity? We need to create new systems and structures that nurture the wellbeing of all people. Companies have a significant role in changing the reality of our world by creating an environment to reach full human potential.

It is worth it to invest in the people of an organization. The benefits to the company are both tangible and intangible. Giving is the new business model to follow. Giving value to everyone is how a company will easily become an Amazing Company!

Whether you choose to work on these elements on your own or by following the Evoloshen System, cracking the amazing code and transforming your company into an Amazing Company can make the difference between fading away or re-birthing to a new level to bring about positive change in the world.

The Evoloshen System will make it fun and easy to implement these changes as we have created The Most Amazing Company Quest. The key steps are laid out in this book like a road map. Working with us will make the implementation a smoother and more fun process for you to follow.

My first word of advice is this: say yes. In fact, say yes as often as you can. Saying yes begins things. Saying yes is how things grow. Saying yes leads to new experiences, and new experiences will lead to knowledge and wisdom. Yes is for young people, and an attitude of yes is how you will be able to go forward in these uncertain times." — *Michael Hogan*

The Most Amazing Company (TMAC) Blueprint

As we have outlined in this book, there is a new way of doing business emerging. We are on a mission to transform organizations to evolve into the new business mindset through engagement. The world needs leaders to step up and embrace a more humanistic, sustainable approach to business. We are passionate about teaching leaders and organizations how to inspire people to maximize their potential and create an Amazing Company.

We believe that life is far too short to settle or, worse, spending it miserably or at work, especially since we spend one third of our lives doing our work. It is possible to create an environment where people can thrive, be productive and filled with joy and excitement about what they are doing. When someone feels good about their work, it naturally spills over into other areas of their lives—they become better spouses, better parents, better friends, and better citizens in general.

We are here to help individuals and organizations reach their full potential and in turn, make a positive difference in the world. Together we can move mountains and create a world where everyone benefits and we can use business as a catalyst to our own global evolution.

How we work with Companies:

Whether an individual, a family, or an organization, all are systems and the answers to better results must begin from within first. It's all about people and bringing more joy into the world! Businesses have the intellectual capital, the systems, and the ability to make huge positive changes in our world by solving global issues that are affecting humanity.

The Evoloshen Program and System is focused on optimizing performance by transforming a workplace into an environment where employees are engaged and thrive. It's a business transformation formula combining all the elements necessary to take your business to a whole new level of growth, profitability, and impact. We have model companies to show the way, and an understanding of the current trends, as well as a deep commitment to transforming the world through new business practices that value, empower, and enhance the people in the organization, the profits, and also the purpose and contribution to the world.

With the Evoloshen Program, we help companies transform and evolve into the next generation of conscious business and help them achieve the high standards of The Most Amazing Company designation.

We inspire companies to create Raving Fans with their employees and customers. We show how happiness increases productivity and bottom line profits.

We help companies:

- Get their employees fully engaged and excited about their work
- Focus on the strengths
- Maintain a higher retention and decrease turnover of employees

- Build better relationships both internally and externally in the company
- Attract the best talent and have a waiting list of incredible people wanting to work for the company
- Have higher engagement and productivity levels because the employees buy into the bigger contribution of the company
- Work with the culture of the company to make it fun to be there for everyone
- Define the values from within so that everyone lives by them
- Be clear on the greater purpose for existence
- Work from within the company to find the unique solutions, values, and create an environment that is stimulating, innovative, creative, collaborative, that allows people to flourish (an environment can be structured to help people to fulfill their potential)
- Create a unique customer experience that instills loyalty, repeat business, and word of mouth marketing
- Teach simple training to rewire the brain to focus on the positive
- And so much more!

Amazing Companies are showing us the way! They know the value of investing in their employees. These companies have much lower employee turnover rates, higher productivity, loyal customers who love them, and higher share holder value. Remember that over a twelve year period, the average shareholder ROI was eleven percent for the companies rated as the Top 100 Best Companies to Work versus three percent for the S&P 500 list of companies.

When disengagement is costing society so much, when the people of a company are what will give you the competitive advantage into the future, when the costs of losing top talent (150 percent minimum per employee) far outweigh the investment in employees (one to three percent of their annual salaries) through recognition and engagement programs, it becomes clear that the solution is right here. Invest in your people and they will bring back a high return. Take care of the employees and they will take care of your customers, your company, and your shareholders. The question one needs to ask is: what are we waiting for?

We have created a program that will take employees from the old industrial mindset and ways of doing business to the new experience and value based models that are transforming the way we do business. Our vision is to see Amazing Companies as the standard; not the exception.

Are you ready to be one?

15

Our Story (as told by Karin)

It's Time To Evolve!

After spending over fifteen years in executive search, and four years going through the biggest personal crisis of my life, I knew I had to make a change in my work to have a bigger impact in the world. But in the beginning of this realization, I had no idea what! Or how!

During our personal crisis, I was forcibly removed from my family and thrown into a very dark world—I was wrongly accused of crimes that my former husband had committed. He was an abusive professional con man and I had been devastated by my first marriage when I discovered everything was based on lies.

When I was put into jail, fighting a legal nightmare that ended up lasting almost four years before I was finally exonerated of all charges, I immersed myself in reading all personal development, scientific, historical, spiritual, religious, and metaphysical material I could get my hands on to survive.

The result of this was that I became stronger and even wrote a series of inspiring children's books for my daughters, called the *Bringing Joy* series, which taught them everything I was learning as well. Our family became empowered and not only survived a major separation but we became even closer and learned to thrive.

When I returned home, I felt a bit lost. I had a deep desire to turn this nightmare experience into something positive. By making a very conscious choice not to be bitter or angry, but rather to teach others how to overcome challenges in their lives, I knew I had a lot to give back to the world. I started working with coaching and mentoring and helping individuals transform their lives.

But I wanted to reach even more people and really empower them to be the best that they can be. Sergio and I have a strong belief in giving of ourselves, of sharing our time, resources, energy and ideas. We have a deep desire to help others. Eventually, this lead to researching companies doing well over the last five years when everyone else seemed to be struggling. We discovered key elements to a new business mindset. This research has lead to writing this book and creating a new business with Evoloshen.

We believe in a new way of doing business—one that focuses on the people and their passions to optimize performance and transform workplaces into environments where employees are engaged and thrive. We called this new brand Evoloshen because we believe that our world is evolving and the ways we do business are too.

We teach leaders and organizations how to inspire people to maximize their potential and work together to create an Amazing Company in a way that is fun and engaging for everyone. We have selected model companies that are the trailblazers in a new business mindset and showing that new business models really do work. They are good for the people and the planet. They make profits that give them the ability to make an even bigger impact in the world.

With Evoloshen, we have created a program and system that evolves companies through engaging their employees—we empower the people to create the fun working environment they desire so that they are excited and engaged at work. Since we spend almost one third of our lives working, it is so important that we love what we do and are able to give the special talent or gift that we are meant to in the world. When everyone in a company is doing that, wonderful things start to happen. Not only to the company—where the productivity and profits are increasing— but also to the employees and their personal lives as well. When people are doing what they love in an environment that they truly enjoy, they become better parents, better spouses, better friends, and better members of their communities.

It's time to evolve how we do business and realize that our companies provide each and every employee the opportunity to shine and thrive. This is good for the people, good for the profits, and great for the planet.

Richard Branson says we can use business as a force for good. We full-heartedly agree and have made it our mission to do just that! Because it's time we evolve to reach our full potential in all ways.

Acknowledgments

Writing this book has not only been a labor of love, it has been a collaborative effort and we could not have done it without the help of so many people. We want to acknowledge and thank our original models of The Most Amazing Companies for showing the way and giving the world the timely inspiration and answers we need: TOMS, Virgin, Zappos, HCL Technologies, PUMA, Whole Foods, Southwest Airlines, MindValley, John Lewis, Achievers, Patagonia, Ben & Jerry's, ElectraWinds, and Misty's Dance. We appreciate the progress all of our interesting companies are making in their journey. (There are so many companies out there that are doing remarkable things, we've only touched on the tip of the iceberg here.) Without the good work you all are doing, this book would have never come to light.

To the enlightened leaders who are taking these companies to a whole new level and raising the stakes in the game, especially Sir Richard Branson, Blake Mycoskie, Tony Hsieh, Vishen Lakhiani, Razor Suleman, Vineet Nayar, Misty Lown, and John McKay.

Also, to all the amazing people we have been able to interview (the list is too long to include here, but you know who you are!)— thank you for sharing so openly and candidly with us. Thanks to all the wonderful authors of the books we have read and been motivated by. We thoroughly enjoyed the company videos and speeches that have inspired us.

And we give a special acknowledgment to all the employees that are out there making the difference in all that they do. Without you, there would be no Amazing Companies nor companies that would be ready to transform.

We are eternally grateful for our fabulous support team who helps keep us sane, and to everyone involved in putting this book together. It truly is a collaborative effort!

Most importantly, we especially want to thank our children for being so supportive for all the dinner table discussions, and the forever late nights and early mornings at the computers. In all that we do, we have you at the center of our hearts!

Appendix A

Appendix A

According to Gallup, there are three main levels of engagement among employees
These components are vital symptoms of a worker's satisfaction

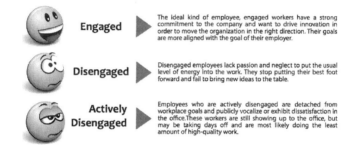

Engaged	The ideal kind of employee, engaged workers have a strong commitment to the company and want to drive innovation in order to move the organization in the right direction. Their goals are more aligned with the goal of their employer.
Disengaged	Disengaged employees lack passion and neglect to put the usual level of energy into the work. They stop putting their best foot forward and fail to bring new ideas to the table.
Actively Disengaged	Employees who are actively disengaged are detached from workplace goals and publicly vocalize or exhibit dissatisfaction in the office. These workers are still showing up to the office, but may be taking days off and are most likely doing the least amount of high-quality work.

When Your Employees Are Appreciated and Captivated at Work!
Productivity Goes Up...

69% of employees say they'd work harder if they felt their efforts were better appreciated and they are even OK with longer commutes. They're more loyal. Those who receive feedback about their strengths have company turnover rates that are 14.9% lower than for employees who received no feedback.

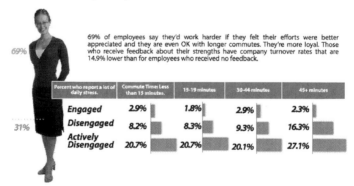

Percent who report a lot of daily stress.	Commute Time: Less than 15 minutes.	15-19 minutes	30-44 minutes	45+ minutes
Engaged	2.9%	1.8%	2.9%	2.3%
Disengaged	8.2%	8.3%	9.3%	16.3%
Actively Disengaged	20.7%	20.7%	20.1%	27.1%

Source: Gallup Wellbeing. "Engaged Workers Immune to Stress From Long Commutes" (2012) Global force Mood Tracker.
"The Impact of Recognition on Employee Retention" (2011) GMJ. "How Strengths Boost Engagement." (2011)

234

The Cure to Office Detachment: A "Job Well Done"

Praise and acknowledgment have been shown to have a more positive effect on employee engagement than financial motivators such as cash bonuses.

Percentage who answered "Very or Extremely Effective"

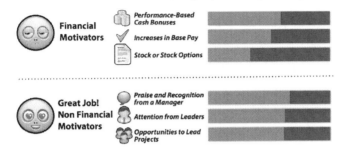

Source: McKinsey Quarterly. "Motivating People, Getting Beyond Money" (2009)

5 Simple Ways to Improve Employee Engagement to Become an Amazing Company!

1. Collaboration

teamwork and trust to empower your people.

2. Creativity

allow for innovation and activity to flow easily

3. Connection

create a deeper connection with employees and customers through values and a thriving culture

4. Celebration

give plenty of recognition and appreciation by focusing on what's going well, have FUN!

5. Contribution

giving back and having a positive impact in the world gives meaning and purpose to your employees - and your company!

To truly engage your employees and increase your productivity and profits, join the Most Amazing Company Quest
www.Evoloshen.com

235

Bibliography

Achor, Shawn. *The Happiness Advantage. The Seven Principles of Positive Psychology That Fuel Success and Performance at Work.* Crown Publishing Group, New York, NY, 2010.

Assaraf, John and Murray Smith. *The Answer.* Atria Books, New York, NY, 2008.

Blanchard, Ken. *Leading at a Higher Level.* Prentice Hall, Upper Saddle River, New Jersey, 2007.

Branson, Richard. *Screw Business as Usual.* Virgin Books, UK, 2011.

Burchard, Brendon. *The Charge.* Free Press, New York, NY, 2012.

Csikszentmihalyi, Mihaly. *Flow—The Psychology of Optimal Experience.* HarperCollins Publishers, New York, NY, 1990.

Csikszentmihalyi, Mihaly, *Creativity, Flow and the Psychology of Discovery and Invention.* HarperCollins Publishers, New York, NY, 1996.

Emmerich, Roxanne. *Thank God it's Monday! How To Create A Workplace You and Your Customers Love.* Pearson Education, FT Press, Upper Saddle River, New Jersey, 2009.

Godin, Seth. *Purple Cow, New Edition: Transform Your Business by Being Remarkable.* Portfolio, New York, NY, 2009.

Godin, Seth. *Tribes: We Need You to Lead Us.* Portfolio , New York, NY, 2008.

Graham, Stedman. *Identity, Your Passion To Success.* Pearson Education, FT Press, Upper Saddle River, New Jersey, 2012.

Hsieh, Tony. *Delivering Happiness—A Path to Profits, Passion, and Purpose.* Business Plus, New York, NY, 2010.

Kaufman, Ron. *Uplifting Service: The Proven Path to Delighting Your Customers, Colleagues, and Everyone Else You Meet.* Evolve Publishing, New York, NY, 2012.

Kofman, Fred. *Conscious Business—How To Build Value Through Values.* Sounds True, Boulder CO, 2006.

Logan, Dave, John King & Halee Fischer-Wright. *Tribal Leadership: Leveraging Natural Groups To Build A Thriving Organization.* Harper-Collins Publishers, New York, NY, 2008.

Mycoskie, Blake. *Start Something That Matters.* Spiegel & Grau, New York, 2012.

MacLeod, David and Nita Clarke. *Engaging For Success: Enhancing Performance Through Employee Engagement.* London: Department for Business, Innovation and Skills, London, UK, 2009.

Nayar, Vineet. *Employees First, Customers Second: Turning Conventional Management Upside Down.* Harvard Business School Publishing, Boston, Massachusetts, 2010.

Pritchett, Price. *You 2: A High-Velocity Formula for Multiplying Your Personal Effectiveness in Quantum Leaps.* Pritchett, Dallas, Texas, 2007.

Ray Paul H. and Sherry Ruth Anderson. *The Cultural Creatives: How 50 Million People Are Changing the World.* Three Rivers Press, New York, NY, 2000.

Seligman, Martin. *Flourish: A Visionary New Understanding of Happiness and Well-Being.* Free Press, New York, NY, 2011.

Sinek, Simon. *Start With Why. How Great Leaders Inspire Everyone to Take Action.* Penguin Group, New York, NY, 2009.

Sisodia, Raj, Jag Sheth & David B. Wolfe. *Firms of Endearment: How World-Class Companies Profit from Passion and Purpose.* Prentice Hall, Upper Saddle River, New Jersey, 2007.

Spence, Roy M. Jr. *It's Not What You Sell, It's What You Stand For... Why Every Extraordinary Business Is Driven By Purpose.* Penguin Group, New York, NY, 2009.

Steward, Henry. *The Happy Manifesto.* Happy, 40 Adler Street, London E1 1EE, 2012.

Endnotes

[1] Sisodia, Raj, Jag Sheth & David B. Wolfe. *Firms of Endearment: How World-Class Companies Profit from Passion and Purpose.* Prentice Hall, Upper Saddle River, New Jersey, 2007 at 4

[2] The General Assembly of the United Nations in its resolution 66/281 of 12 July 2012

[3] Kelly, Annie. *Gross national happiness in Bhutan: the big idea from a tiny state that could change the world.* The Observer. December1, 2012.

[4] Kjerulf, Alexander. *Top 10 reasons why happiness at work is the ultimate productivity booster.* Retrieved March 27, 2007 from http://positivesharing.com

[5] Seligman, Martin, *Flourish: A Visionary New Understanding of Happiness and Well-Being,* Free Press, New York, NY, 2011 at 16

[6] *The Business Impact of Talent Intelligence*, Human Capital Institute, 2012. Retrieved from http://www.ikgundemi.com/uploads/6/7/8/0/6780997/2012_taleo_intelligence_229.pdf

[7] Smith, Gregory P. *The Cost of Employee Turnover,* PHCC Educational Foundation, July 9, 2007.

[8] Turnover (employment) Wikipedia. Retrieved from http://en.wikipedia.org/wiki/Turnover_%28employment%29

[9] *New Research Shows Training Yields Major Benefits to Business*, National Centre for Vocational Education Research, December 11, 2001.

[10] *Canadian Companies Having Difficulty Attracting Critical-Skill Employees*, Towers Watson Survey Finds. Towers Watson Talent Management and Rewards Survey, October 2011.

[11] *Facing the talent challenge.* PricewaterhouseCoopers 15th Annual Global CEO Survey, 2012. Retrieved from http://www.pwc.com/gx/en/ceo-survey/key-findings/hr-talent-strategies.jhtml

[12] *Survey Finds Wide Employee Discontent.* Right Management, November 29, 2011. Retrieved from http://www.right.com/news-and-events/press-releases/2011-press-releases/item22035.aspx

[13] Martin, Judy. *10 Reasons The Human Capital Zeitgeist Is Emerging.* Forbes, March 19, 2012. Retrieved from http://www.forbes.com/sites/work-in-progress/2012/03/19/10-reasons-the-human-capital-zeitgeist-is-emerging/

[14] Alleyne,Richard. *Welcome to the information age – 174 newspapers a day.* The Telegraph, February 11, 2011.

[15] Meyer, Christopher,Ray Kurzweil. *2003 The Cap Gemini Ernst & Young Center for Business Innovation.*

[16] *Create an Attractive Workplace. Source: Building Better Workplaces. Retrieved from* http://www.nlhrmanager.ca

[17] Declaration of Interdependence at www.wholefoodsmarket.com

[18] Ransom, Diana. *Finding Success by Putting Company Culture First.* Entrepreneur. April 19, 2011.

[19] Robbins, Mel. *F— YOU - How To Stop Screwing Yourself Over.* TEDxSF Talk from June 11, 2011 retrieved from http://www.youtube.com/watch?v=Lp7E973zozc.

[20] Gerloff ,Dr. Pamela. *Are You Meeting Your Laugh Quota? Why You Should Laugh Like a 5-Year-Old*, The Possibility Paradigm, June 21, 2011.

[21] Achievers, *The 2013 Guide to Recognition* Slideshare presentation posted on *Mar 18, 2013. Retrieved from http://ggu.libguides.com/content. php?pid=61377&sid=453561.*

[22] *Southwest blog.* Funny Stuff..., June 9m 2006. Retrieved from http://www.blogsouthwest.com/2006/06/09/funny-stuff

[23] Hsieh, Tony. Delivering Happiness, *A Path to Profits, Passion, and Purpose.* Business Plus, New York, NY, 2010 at 154.

[24] Who Gives A Crap - First Edition. July 9, 2012. Retrieved from http://www.youtube.com/watch?v=WdWZ8WVv6qk

[25] Hammond, Jeffrey S. *Case Study: HCL Technologies Puts Employees First, Customers Second*, Forrester Research, August 22, 2011,at 4-5.

[26] Denning, Steve. *Valuing Employees (Really!): Lessons from India*, Forbes, May 10, 2011.

[27] Speech *"Leadership The Virgin Way"*, delivered by Tony Collins CEO Virgin Trains, provided by Arthur Leathley, Director of Communications.

[28] Sisodia, Raj, Jag Sheth & David B. Wolfe. *Firms of Endearment: How World-Class Companies Profit from Passion and Purpose.* Prentice Hall, Upper Saddle River, New Jersey, 2007 at 201.

[29] Kahney, Leander. *How Apple Got Everything Right By Doing Everything Wrong.* Wired Magazine, March 18, 2008.

[30] Steward, Henry. *The Happy Manifesto.* Happy, Clays Ltd, St Ives plc, London UK, 2012 at 9.

[31] Gallup Report, 2013. *The State of The American Workplace, Employee Engagement Insights for U.S. Business Leaders.* Retrieved from http://www.gallup.com/strategicconsulting/163007/state-american-workplace.aspx

[32] Gallup Report, 2013. Ibid.

[33] Towers Perrin-ISR(2006) The ISR Employee Engagement Report

[34] Gallup, 2003, cited in Melcrum (2005), Employee Engagement: How to Build A High Performance Workforce.

[35] CBI –Axa (2007), Annual Absence and Labour Turnover Survey.

[36] Gallup Report 2013, ibid.

[37] Right Management (2006), *Measuring True Employee Engagement*, A CIPD Report.

[38] Corporate leadership council, corporate executive Board. *Driving Performance and Retention Through Employee Engagement: a quantitative analysis of effective engagement strategies.* 2004.

[39] MacLeod, D. and Clarke, N. (2009). *Engaging for success: Enhancing Performance Through Employee Engagement.* London: Department for Business, Innovation and Skills.

[40] Gallup Report 2013, ibid.

[41] Gallup 2003, ibid.

[42] Barsade, S. (2002). *The ripple effect: Emotional contagion and its influence on group behavior.* Administrative Science Quarterly, *47, 644–677.*

[43] Strategy + Business. *The Global Innovation 1000: Why Culture Is Key*, Oct 2011.

[44] ComPsych Survey. *Employees Report They Are Too Stressed to Be Effective, According to ComPsych Survey.* Press Releases, October 25, 2011.

[45] Martin, Judy. *10 Reasons The Human Capital Zeitgeist Is Emerging.* Forbes, March 19, 2012.

[46] Lakhiani, Vishen. Why Happiness is the New Productivity (The Story of Mindvalley). Retrieved from http://www.mindvalley.com/flow.

[47] Brush, Candida. *Closing the Gender Gap for Women Entrepreneurs,* Forbes, May 5 2012.

[48] *The American Psychological Association Washington, D.C. APA Survey Finds Feeling Valued at Work Linked to Well-Being and Performance. Press releases,* March 8, 2012.

[49] *'United Breaks Guitars': Did It Really Cost The Airline $180 Million?,* Huffington Post, August 8, 2009.

[50] Abercrombie & Fitch Gets a Brand Readjustment #FitchTheHomeless. Retrieved from https://www.youtube.com/watch?v=O95DBxnXiSo

[51] Bodyform Responds: The Truth. Retrieved from https://www.youtube.com/watch?v=Bpy75q2DDow and http://www.youtube.com/watch?annotation_id=annotation_903195&feature=iv&src_vid=Bpy75q2DDow&v=1GRi59CfJqI

[52] *Don't Believe Facebook; You Only Have 150 Friends,* NPR Staff, NPR, June 05, 2011.

[53] Sisodia, Raj, Jag Sheth & David B. Wolfe . *Firms of Endearment. How World-Class Companies Profit from Passion and Purpose.* Prentice Hall, Upper Saddle River, New Jersey, 2007 at 198.

[54] Jacques Bughin and Michael Chui. *The rise of the networked enterprise: Web 2.0 finds its payday, McKinsey Quarterly,* December 2010.

[55] Bontis, Dr. Nick. Institute for Intellectual Capital Research (ICR), 1998.

[56] Coleman, David. *Profitable Collaboration for SMB,* Collaborative Strategies. July 21 2011.

[57] Glanz, Barbara A. *Care Packages for the Workplace: Dozens of Little Things You Can Do to Regenerate Spirit at Work.* New York, McGraw Hill, and with Ken Blanchard, *The Simple Truths of Service Inspired by Johnny the Bagger®.* Chicago, IL, Simple Truths. Contact Barbara at www.barbaraglanz.com

[58] Bryant, Adam. *Google's Quest to Build a Better Boss,* The New York Times, March 12, 2011.

[59] Goleman, Daniel. *What Makes A Leader?,* Harvard Business Review, January 2004. Retrieved from http://hbr.org/2004/01/what-makes-a-leader

[60] Stephen Bernhut (2002). *"Primal Leadership, with Daniel Goleman,"* Ivey Business Journal, May/June, Volume 66, Issue 5, pp. 14–15. 29.

[61] Brian Tracy, *The Seven Leadership Qualities of Great Leaders,* www.BrianTracy.com/blog , December 17, 2012.

[62] Branson, Richard. *Screw Business As Usual.* Virgin Books. London, UK. 2011.

[63] Pink, Daniel. The Puzzle of Motivation TED Talk. TEDGlobal 2009. Retrieved from http://www.ted.com/talks/dan_pink_on_motivation.html.

[64] http://en.wikipedia.org/wiki/Nordstrom

[65] *http://www.wholefoodsmarket.com/mission-values/core-values/declaration-interdependence*

[66] Sisodia, Raj, Jag Sheth & David B. Wolfe. *Firms of Endearment. How World-Class Companies Profit from Passion and Purpose.* Prentice Hall, Upper Saddle River, New Jersey, 2007 pp 123

[67] http://www.waitrosejobs.com/about-us/partnership-spirit.htm

[68] *The Economic Case for People Performance Management* and Measurement. The Forum for People Performance Management and Measurement. Retrieved from http://www.incentivecentral.org/business_motivation/whitepapers/the_economic_case_for_ppmm.2038.html

[69] Achievers. *The 2013 Guide to Recognition: How To Create A Strategy That Drives Employee Success.* 2013. p.9.

[70] Tabaka, Marla. *Simple Trick to Update Your Marketing.* Inc, June 4, 2012.

[71] www.ZeroMomentofTruth.com

[72] McNeil, Gary and Robert Spector. *The Nordstrom Way To Customer Service Excellence.* SlideShare presentation. Retrieved from http://www.slideshare.net/parature/the-nordstrom-way-to-customer-service-excellence .

[73] Sharma, Robin. *The Rare Art of Customer Delight.* www.RobinSharma.com/blog March 7, 2011.

[74] Pierce, Kathleen. *Disgruntled patrons get Ben & Jerry's inside scoop.* BostonGlobe, March 11, 2013.

[75] Interview with Kelly Mohr, Asst. Manager of PR Shenanigans at Ben & Jerry's, April 3, 2013.

[76] Semuels, Alana. *Rejecting industry dogma, Costco backs calls to lift minimum wage.* Los Angeles Times, March 06, 2013

[77] http://www.johnlewispartnership.co.uk/about/the-partnership-spirit.html

[78] Martin, Judy. *10 reasons the human capital zeitgeist is emerging.* Forbes, March 19, 2012.

[79] Kerby, Rob. *Wild elephants gather inexplicably, mourn death of "Elephant Whisperer",* Beliefnet.com, May 2012. Retrieved from http://www.beliefnet.com/Inspiration/Home-Page-News-and-Views/Wild-Elephants-Mourn-Death-of-famed-Elephant-Whisperer.aspx

[80] Sisodia, Raj, Jag Sheth & David B. Wolfe. *Firms of Endearment. How World-Class Companies Profit from Passion and Purpose.* Prentice Hall, Upper Saddle River, New Jersey, 2007, pp 20.

[81] TOMS Giving Report. Retrieved from http://www.readbag.com/toms-media-files-8-24-11-givingreport-update pp3.

[82] Norton, Michael. *How To Buy Happiness.* TEDx Cambridge, November 2011. Retrieved from http://www.ted.com/talks/michael_norton_how_to_buy_happiness.html

Join the next TMAC Quest and become a Most Amazing Company

Application Details at
www.TheMostAmazingCompany.com

Because we believe in a new way of doing business!

About the Authors

Karin Volo is the **Evolution Expert** specializing in engagement and in personal and corporate development. With over fifteen years experience working with international Fortune 500 companies on two continents, she has gained insights on business building, cultural transformation, and high performance. Karin has worked with executive search, leadership mentoring, as well as professional inspirational speaking. She uses her professional skills and draws from her personal experiences to help individuals and companies thrive through difficult transitions. Her passion is empowering and evolving businesses with a people first approach that promotes engagement and change. Her mission is bringing joy to the world!

Sergio Volo is the **Visionary Transformation Facilitator** specializing in corporate culture and leadership. He has a talent for finding the uniqueness in each person or organization and seeing the possibilities of transformation. With over twenty years working with international companies with business development, HR systems, and executive search and coaching, he is an expert at seeing the opportunities and helping maximize potential through people engagement. His clients say he is passionate, determined, committed, and innovative. His passion is commitment to success and creating new ways of doing business to sustain productivity and profitability. His natural talent is to see the path and make things happen!

Made in the USA
Charleston, SC
15 September 2013